# Mary Stuart's Scotland

MARIA D·G· SCOTIÆ REGINA, GALLIÆ DOTARIA, MAII 17·1568· AVXILII AB ELISABETHA PROMISSI SPE ET OPINIONE DESCENDIT IN ANGLIAM· VBI CONTRA IVS GENTIVM, ET FOEDERIS IVRATI FIDEM, ANNOS VNDEVIGINTI RETENTA, TANDEM HOSPITIS ELISABETHÆ PARRICIDIO CHRISTI MARTYRIBVS ADDITA, SANGVINIS LIBERALITER EFFVSI TESTIMONIO DEI LEGITIMVM CVLTV, ET ECCLESIÆ ROMANÆ FIDEM PROFESSA, CORONAM MERVIT IN CŒLIS, ILLIS TRIBVS ILLVSTRIOREM, QVARV VSVM VIOLENTER AMISIT IN TERRIS· 18· FEBRVAR 1587·

# Mary Stuart's Scotland

The landscapes, life and legends
of Mary Queen of Scots

## David and Judy Steel

with photographs by Eric Thorburn

WEIDENFELD AND NICOLSON · LONDON

First published in Great Britain in 1987 by
George Weidenfeld and Nicolson Ltd
91 Clapham High Street
London SW4 7TA

ISBN 0 297 79073 0

Picture research by Robert Turnbull
Designed by Joy FitzSimmons, assisted by Sheila Sherwen

Colour separations by Newsele Litho Ltd
Typeset by Keyspools Ltd
Printed and bound in Italy

# CONTENTS

Introduction  6

Principal Characters in Mary Stuart's Scotland  8

Principal Events in Mary Stuart's Scotland  9

1  The Inheritance: Renaissance Scotland  12

2  The Birthplace: Linlithgow  26

3  The Nursery: Stirling  32

4  The Place of Safety: Dumbarton  40

5  Edinburgh: Port and Castle  48

6  Edinburgh: Town and Palace  62

7  Fife: Playground of Royalty  76

8  The North: Quelling an Uprising  86

9  The Maries: Homes and Families  94

10  Friends and Relations: Homes and Families  106

11  The Borders: Living Dangerously  116

12  The Lothians: Bothwell's Territory  126

13  Lochleven: Familiar Prison  138

14  The South-West: Point of Departure  148

Acknowledgments  156
Index  157

# INTRODUCTION

After the warm reception of our book on the Borders, George Weidenfeld asked us to follow it up with a second one dealing with another part of Scotland. It was my friend John Matthews, who lives in Linlithgow, who made the suggestion that forms the subject matter of this book. Our first thanks go to him.

It was a good, logical idea, though he had related it only to David's student years in Linlithgow, when his father was minister of the church in which Mary Queen of Scots was baptized. But then it dawned on us how much of our lives had been spent in the places most associated with her. David had spent boyhood years in Dumbarton and in Fife; I was born in the shadow of Castle Campbell in Dollar, home of her sister and one of the many castles that welcomed her within its doors. My adolescence was spent near Stirling, whose fortress-like palace saw the infant years of Queen Mary. The streets and wynds of Old Edinburgh are dear and familiar to us, and from time to time we are lucky enough to see the inside of Edinburgh Castle and Holyrood Palace on grand and glittering state occasions. The Border hills where she hunted, and over which she made her way to visit the wounded Bothwell, have been our home for over twenty years (indeed, I had planned to take part in the commemorative ride to Hermitage two decades ago – but recent childbirth prevented me). In short, we felt able to identify in some way with nearly every part of Mary's Scotland. And the combination of my obsession with pre-union Scottish history and the magnetism that draws David to old (and preferably ruined) buildings seemed to make it an ideal project for us.

We have encountered a lot of difficulties, the first and major one being lack of time. Our re-visiting of old haunts throughout Scotland – and the discovery of new ones – was crammed into the summer parliamentary recess. Another was my assumption that most people would already have a detailed knowledge of Mary Stuart, either through the extensive bibliography of fact, or the equally great one of fiction; and that earlier history such as the Scottish Wars of Independence, the Renaissance and the Reformation were general knowledge. David's view was that only a minority of readers would have such information. I hope, therefore, that the background sketches tread the middle path between faintness and fussiness. The history of Scotland in Mary's century was complicated and depended much on events abroad (including those in England); and the task of relating it to individual buildings and areas without becoming irritatingly repetitive has not been easy. But I hope that each chapter – taken with the initial information following this introduction – can stand on its own.

Another difficulty is that it is simply not possible to be objective about Mary. Everyone who takes a view on her must find their own answer, on their own interpretation of the evidence, to two questions: was she implicated in Darnley's murder? and did she connive with Bothwell's abduction of her to Dunbar? From one's answer to these questions all other judgements on her follow. Everyone is an individual juror, and one's verdict can only be made – as in a civil court – on the balance of probabilities, and not, as in a criminal trial, on proof beyond reasonable doubt. Perhaps, appropriately enough, the Scots 'not proven' verdict is as correct as any. That is ours. But the reader may have his or her preconceptions, and believe that the passionate casket letters *were* in fact penned by Mary to Bothwell at the height of an adulterous and homicidal love affair. And he or she could well be right. That is the enigma, and the fascination.

Mary leaves a distorted view of her times, for such concerns overshadow the more serious and equally interesting events. The significance of men like Knox and Moray and Maitland dims beside her transient glamour, and their characters are given short shrift by her hagiographers and by the novelists. But she acts as a catalyst in attracting worldwide attention to a few years of Scottish history, which can only be good. (I write this after returning from Leningrad, where a modern and historically sound – if musically controversial – opera based on her Scottish years has played to full houses over a three-year period.)

We have dealt only with our own country, of which she was the anointed sovereign, and have not attempted to trace her years in France or England. Our hope is simply that in enjoying the pages of this book, readers will want to explore the rich and varied heritage to which she succeeded, and which is so often grossly neglected today.

In the preparation of this book, we have been fortunate in our collaboration with Eric Thorburn and his wife Lis. Eric's photography is well known in Scotland, and we have admired it for many years.

Two people deserve particular thanks: Vicky Davidson, who was present when John Matthews conceived the idea, who researched the chapters on Stirling and Edinburgh, and whose enthusiasm has often kept ours from flagging; and Barbara Mellor, whose patience in editing out-of-sequence and badly typed chapters was never-ending.

Many other people have helped and encouraged us: my sister Fay Black, who made all the Fife research so enjoyable; David's father, the Very Rev. Dr David Steel, whose deep knowledge of Dumbarton and Linlithgow stood us in good stead; Elspeth Campbell, who furnished us with many leads, especially in East Lothian; Peter and Flora Maxwell Stuart of Traquair; Peter and Janet Wright, who are masterminding the ambitious Niddry Castle restoration; Rosie Capper, Curator of Roxburgh Museums, under whose lead Queen Mary's house in Jedburgh has become a fitting heritage centre; Michael Ambrose, Director of the Borders Tourist Board, and, coincidentally and invaluably for us, Chairman of the Mary Queen of Scots co-ordinating committee; Miss Martha Hamilton, headmistress of St Leonard's School; the staff of the Borders Regional Library; and helpful curators and guides everywhere.

Judy Steel
*Ettrick Bridge, October 1986*

# PRINCIPAL CHARACTERS
# IN MARY STUART'S SCOTLAND

MARY STEWART (later Stuart), Queen of Scots

*Her parents*
James V (died 1542)
Mary of Guise or Lorraine (died 1560)

*Her father's first wife*
Princess Madeleine of France

*His principal mistress*
Margaret Erskine, Lady Douglas of Lochleven (mother
   of Lord James Stewart)

*Mary's husbands*
(1) The Dauphin (later Francis II) of France
(2) Henry Stuart, Lord Darnley
(3) James Hepburn, fourth Earl of Bothwell

*Her parents-in-law*
(1) Henri II of France and Catherine de Medici
(2) Matthew, fourth Earl of Lennox, and Lady Margaret
   Douglas, half-sister to James V
(3) Patrick, third Earl of Bothwell (died 1556) and Lady
   Agnes Sinclair

*Her half-siblings (illegitimate offspring of James V)*
Lord James Stewart (later Earl of Moray), political leader
   of the Protestant party
Lord John Stewart
Lord Robert Stewart
Jean, Countess of Argyll

*Her governess and aunt*
Janet, Lady Fleming (illegitimate half-sister to James V)

*Her guardians*
The fifth Lord Erskine
The fifth Lord Livingstone

*Governor of Scotland and 'second person' to the crown during
   Mary's early minority*
James Hamilton, second Earl of Arran (later Duke of
   Châtelherault)

*Her son by Darnley*
Prince James, later James VI of Scotland and I of
   England

*His guardian*
The sixth Lord Erskine (later Earl of Mar)

*Leading Protestants*
John Knox, religious leader of the Scottish Reformation
George Wishart, martyr (died 1546)
The third Earl of Arran
The fifth Earl of Argyll
Lord Ruthven
Lord Lindsay
Sir William Kirkcaldy of Grange, soldier
John Cockburn of Ormiston, East Lothian laird
George Buchanan, scholar

*Leading Catholics, or those especially loyal to Mary's party*
Cardinal David Beaton (died 1546)
The fourth Earl of Huntly (died 1562)
The fifth Earl of Huntly
The fifth Lord Seton
The sixth Lord Livingstone
The fifth Lord Fleming
The Master of Maxwell (later Lord Herries)
Sir Walter Scott of Buccleuch

*Prominent members of Mary's court*
Mary Fleming (daughter of fourth Lord Fleming, later
   Lady Maitland of Lethington)
Mary Livingstone (daughter of fifth Lord Livingstone)
Mary Seton (daughter of fourth Lord Seton)
Mary Beaton (daughter of Robert Beaton of Creich)
Sir William Maitland of Lethington, Secretary of State
David Rizzio, Italian musician and private secretary
Pierre de Châtelard, French poet
Sir James Melville
Sir Simon Preston of Craigmillar, Provost of Edinburgh
Sir John Stewart of Traquair
Sir Thomas Randolph, English Ambassador and gossip
   columnist

# PRINCIPAL EVENTS
# IN MARY STUART'S SCOTLAND

**1542**

November: Defeat of Scots army by English at Solway Moss.

December: Birth of Mary at Linlithgow Palace. Death of James V; one-week old Mary becomes queen.

**1543**

Earl of Arran appointed Governor by Scots Parliament, against opposition from Mary of Guise and Cardinal Beaton. Arran signs treaty with Henry VIII of England, the terms of which include Mary's marriage to Henry's son Prince Edward. Treaty overthrown: Mary removed to Stirling Castle. English troops invade the Borders, and the 'rough wooing' begins. Earl of Lennox returns to Scotland from France.

**1544–5**

Further invasions of Scotland via Leith and the Borders by troops under the Earl of Hertford and Lord Wharton. Widespread destruction in southern Scotland. Earl of Lennox defects to Henry VIII and marries his niece Margaret Douglas.

**1546**

The Protestant preacher George Wishart martyred. Cardinal Beaton murdered in reprisal, and St Andrews Castle occupied by militant supporters of the Reformation.

**1547**

Death of Henry VIII. Scots army defeated by English troops under Protector Somerset at Pinkie Cleugh. Mary removed temporarily to Inchmahome Priory. South-east Scotland under English occupation. St Andrews Castle captured by French: John Knox and others taken prisoner.

**1548**

Mary removed to Dumbarton Castle. Henri II of France agrees to send help. The Treaty of Haddington agrees to Mary's marriage to the Dauphin and Scotland's acceptance of the 'protection' of the French king. Arran becomes Duke of Châtelherault. Mary leaves Dumbarton for France, and French troops oust the English.

**1550**

Mary of Guise visits her daughter in France.

**1554**

Mary of Guise becomes Governor of Scotland.

**1557**

The gathering strength of the Reformation in Scotland leads to the 'Lords of the Congregation' signing their first bond.

**1558**

Marriage of Mary to the Dauphin Francis. By a secret treaty she bequeaths Scotland to the French crown.

Death of Mary Tudor: Elizabeth succeeds to the English throne, and re-establishes Protestantism there.

Lord James Stewart joins the Lords of the Congregation.

### 1559

John Knox returns to Scotland and establishes himself as the figurehead of the Reformation. Death of Henri II of France – Mary and Francis succeed to the throne, but are under the influence of Mary's Guise uncles. Rebellion against Mary of Guise's pro-Catholic, pro-French policy gathers strength, aided by Elizabeth. Bothwell refuses to join his fellow Protestants in rebellion, and intercepts money from Elizabeth for their cause.

### 1560

The siege of Leith ends in victory for allied troops of Scots Protestants and English over supporters of Mary of Guise. Treaty of Leith ends 250-year-old alliance between Scotland and France. Death of Mary of Guise at Edinburgh Castle.

'Reformation' parliament passes various measures including the banning of Mass. Scotland governed by a triumvirate of Châtelherault, his son Arran, and Lord James Stewart.

Death of Francis II.

### 1561

Protestant rule gains in authority.

August: Mary lands in Scotland at Leith and takes up residence in Holyrood Palace. In September, she makes her first 'progress' through Stirling, Perth, Dundee and Fife.

### 1562

Marriage of Lord James. Mary enobles him as Earl of Mar and (secretly) of Moray.

Mary makes a protracted visit to St Andrews: Bothwell is implicated by Arran in a plot to kidnap her. He is imprisoned, but later escapes. Arran is declared insane.

Mary pursues a policy of conciliation with the Protestants, aided by Moray. In the autumn the rebellion of Huntly takes her to the north-east, as far as Inverness. Huntly is defeated, and dies at the battle of Corrichie.

### 1563

Stable rule in Scotland as Mary continues to work in partnership with Moray and Maitland. Far-reaching legislation against personal immorality passed. The poet Châtelard compromises Mary, and is executed at St Andrews. Mary makes a pilgrimage to the south-west.

### 1564

The political situation continues smoothly, but Mary gives up hope of a foreign marriage. The Earl of Lennox returns to Scotland.

Mary appoints David Rizzio as a musician, and then as private secretary. She meets her cousin, Henry, Lord Darnley.

### 1565

Mary marries Darnley against opposition from Moray. Bothwell is recalled from exile. A rebellion by Moray results in his rout (the 'Chaseabout Raid') and flight to England, via Dumfries.

Mary becomes pregnant, and Darnley's behaviour begins to destroy the marriage and cause hostility amongst the lords.

### 1566

Bothwell marries Lady Jean Gordon.

Nobles, led by Lord Ruthven, involve Darnley in a plot to murder Rizzio in Mary's presence, offering him power after a *coup d'état*. The murder takes place and Moray returns. Mary, heavily pregnant, subverts Darnley and with Bothwell's assistance they escape to Dunbar. Mary returns to Edinburgh in triumph, and is superficially reconciled to Moray.

Birth of Prince James at Edinburgh Castle. Mary and Darnley appear to be finally estranged. Bothwell's influence grows. In the autumn, Mary sets off with Moray for the Borders to administer justice. They visit Bothwell, who is wounded, at Hermitage Castle, and afterwards Mary comes near to death at Jedburgh.

In November, at Craigmillar, she discusses a divorce. A bond is signed by Bothwell and other nobles to eliminate Darnley.

In December Prince James is baptized at Stirling.

## 1567

Darnley, intriguing in Glasgow, falls ill. Mary takes him to Kirk o'Field in Edinburgh. The house is destroyed by an explosion, and Darnley is strangled. Placards accuse Bothwell of the murder and implicate Mary.

Bothwell stands trial at Lennox's instance, but no evidence is given. He abducts Mary to Dunbar, obtains a divorce and marries her.

General outrage at the marriage results in widespread rebellion.

Mary and Bothwell fail to rally support and surrender at Carberry Hill. Bothwell leaves, is outlawed, and finds his way to Denmark where he is kept in custody.

Mary is imprisoned in Lochleven. She is forced to abdicate, and Moray becomes Regent. The casket letters are found, apparently confirming her complicity in Darnley's murder. murder.

## 1568

Mary escapes from Lochleven and gathers support. Her troops are defeated by Moray's, and she makes her way via the south-west to England, and imprisonment rather than sanctuary.

# 1

# THE INHERITANCE: RENAISSANCE SCOTLAND

There is a charm in footing slow across a silent plain,
Where patriot battle has been fought, where glory had the gain:
There is a pleasure on the heath where druids old have been,
Where mantles grey have rustled by and swept the nettles green.
There is a deeper joy than all, more piercing to the heart,
More parching to the soul than all, of more divine a smart,
When weary steps forget themselves upon a pleasant turf,
Upon hot sand, or dusty road, or sea shore's iron surf
Towards the castle or the cot, where long ago was born
One who was great through mortal days, and died of fame unshorn.

*A figure at Falkland Palace in Fife, the epitome of Scottish Renaissance architecture built by Queen Mary's father, James V.*

So wrote John Keats after a visit to the birthplace of Robert Burns in 1818, and his lines hold good for places explored in this volume too. People are drawn to places and buildings as much by their association with the past as by their natural or architectural splendour; and nowhere in Scotland is this more true than with the places that give us a tangible link with the romantic and tragic figure of Mary Queen of Scots.

This is all the more remarkable in view of the fact that she spent longer in France, in gilded and sheltered childhood, and in England, in ever increasing discomfort and isolation, than she did in her own land. She never visited the remote western parts of the Highlands and islands, and many of the places alleged to have been her resting place for the occasional night found their claims on tradition rather than evidence. Indeed, the majority of places with which she is associated have their own long and eventful histories, of which she is only one brief episode.

Yet how many visitors would take the time to sail across the Lake of Menteith to the ruins of the lovely thirteenth-century priory of Inchmahome, were it not for the three-week visit of the child queen, seeking refuge after the Scottish defeat at Pinkie Cleugh in 1547? And the stout walls of Hermitage Castle in Liddesdale, like other Border keeps, have borne the brunt of many an attack, and witnessed many poignant tragedies. But it is not in the main part the tales of those attacks and tragedies that draw people so many miles down the winding roads from Jedburgh or Hawick: they come to see the place which one wet October day in 1566 was the destination of Mary Queen of Scots and her party of courtiers, who came to visit the wounded Bothwell. The glamour she casts on all these places is enhanced rather than erased by the passage of time.

They also speak volumes about the kind of Scotland she inherited, and about the history of a nation which had painfully kept its independence intact over the centuries and which, through the accidents of royal marriages, premature deaths, and lack of fertility, was destined for absorption by – rather than union with – its traditional enemy.

At the beginning of Mary's century, Scotland was at one of its highest points. The portrait too often painted of Scotland as a backward nation, away from the mainstream of events, was never more untrue. James IV, strong, able and popular, had governed for twelve years. He had ascended the throne without a damaging period of minority, and had proceeded to draw together under his authority the various noble houses who had jostled for position throughout the previous century. He had established order on the frequently unruly Border as well as mastery in fact as well as name over the semi-autonomous Highlands and islands. To do this he had not only travelled throughout the land but had also taken the time and trouble to learn Gaelic. His was a triumph of diplomacy as well as of force. He was also fortunate in that to the north and east he could count on the friendship of the King of Denmark (his mother was a Danish princess), and a busy trade route between the east coast and the Low Countries ensured a community of interest there; and of course there were the traditional ties with France. But, most important, the situation to the south promised peace on that vulnerable flank. The conclusion of the destructive Wars of the Roses found Henry VII triumphant but vulnerable. He was too preoccupied with establishing himself and his descendants on the throne of England to start reactivating dubious territorial claims on Scotland. He forgave James some initially rash behaviour, for example when the latter supported the claims of the impostor Perkin Warbeck to Henry's new throne; and in time he was able to offer a valuable pawn to his northern neighbour: his daughter Margaret in marriage.

It is unlikely that either monarch imagined that the result of this would be the eventual merging of the kingdoms. Henry, after all, had two sons, both older than Margaret, with the prospect of more. The marriage, in 1503, was simply meant to indicate friendly relations with a foreign power, and was celebrated with great rejoicing and extravagance. At that time Henry VII's court was austere, while James's hummed with the ideas and artistic excitement of a Renaissance court. William Dunbar, chief of the vibrant school of Scottish poets of the time, celebrated the event in a poem entitled 'The Marriage of the Thistle and the Rose':

> Upon the awful thistle she did look
> And saw him, guarded with a bush of spears
> Considering him so able for the wars,
> A radiant crown of rubies she him gave,
> And said, 'In field go forth and guard the rest.
>
> 'Nor hold no other flower in such dainty
> As the fresh rose, of colour red and white:
> For if thou dost, hurt is thine honesty;
> Considering that no flower is so perfect
> So full of virtue, pleasance and delight,
> So full of blissful angelic beauty,
> Imperial birth, honour and dignity.'

It was not just the king who gave encouragement to learning and to the arts. Nobles like Lord Sinclair, whose patronage allowed Gavin Douglas to translate Virgil's *Aeneid* into Scots, followed his example. The church, too, played a major part, especially in fostering the development of music. Scotland was *not* a country of primitive tunes played on bagpipes and little else besides. Choir schools flourished, supported by both church and burgh; viol consorts were formed; organs were installed. Scottish musicians travelled to Flanders, France and England to widen their knowledge and refine their technique.

In the field of education Scotland was already in the forefront. While England, a larger country, had two universities, Scotland had three – at St Andrews, Glasgow and Aberdeen – all of them episcopal foundations. The last-named was founded in the reign of James IV,

BELOW *This beautifully carved niche survives among the ruins of Melrose Abbey. Religious foundations such as Melrose had played a significant part in the life of Scotland over the centuries, contributing to artistic as well as spiritual life. But by the start of Mary's reign the internal state of the church was influencing the progress of the Reformation.*

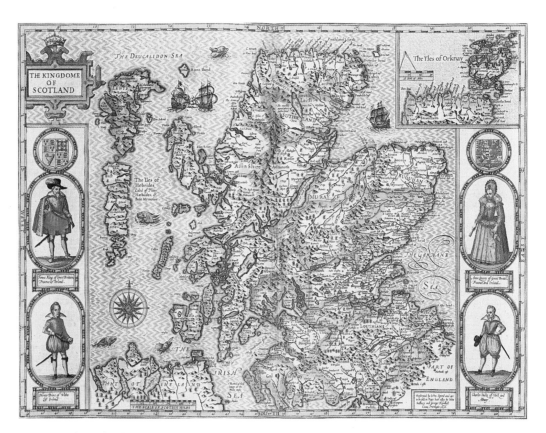

RIGHT *Sixteenth-century Scotland as it appeared to contemporary cartographers.*

very much under his influence. By the turn of the century it had become compulsory for all barons and householders to send their eldest sons to grammar school and 'to keep them there till they have perfect Latin'.

Peace internally; peace externally: a contemporary portrait by the Spanish ambassador Pedro de Ayala gives us a glimpse of the man who achieved it:

He is of noble stature, neither tall nor short, and as handsome in the complexion and shape as a man can be. His address is very agreeable. He speaks the following foreign languages: Latin, very well; French, German, Flemish, Italian and Spanish; Spanish as well as the Marquis, but he pronounces it more distinctly. His own Scottish language is as different from the English as Aragonese from Castilian. The king speaks, besides, the languages of the savages who live in some parts of Scotland and on the islands. It is as different from Scottish as Biscayan is from Castilian. His knowledge of languages is wonderful. He is well read in the Bible and other devout books. He is a good historian. He had read many Latin and French histories, and has profited by them, as he has a very good memory. He never cuts his hair or beard: it becomes him very well. He fears God and observes all the precepts of the church. He does not eat meat on Wednesdays or Fridays. He would not ride on Sundays for any consideration, not even to Mass. He says all his prayers. Before transacting any business, he hears two masses. After Mass he has a cantata sung, during which he sometimes despatches very urgent business. He gives alms liberally; but is a severe judge, especially in the case of murderers. He has a great predilection for priests, and receives advice from them, especially from the Friars Observant, with whom he confesses.

Rarely, even in joking, does a word escape him that is not the truth. He prides himself much on it, and says it does not seem to him well for kings to swear their treaties as they do now. The oath of a king should be his royal word, as was the case in bygone days. He is neither prodigal nor avaricious, but liberal when occasion demands. He is courageous, even more so than a king should be. I am a good witness of it. I have often seen him undertake most dangerous things in the last wars. On such occasions he does not take good care of himself. He is not a good captain, because he begins to fight before he has given his orders. He said to me that his subjects serve him with their persons and goods,

in just and unjust quarrels, exactly as he likes, and that therefore he does not think it right to begin any warlike undertaking without being himself first in the danger. His deeds are as good as his words. For this reason, and because he is a very humane prince, he is much loved. He is active, and works hard.

When he is not at war he hunts in the mountains. I tell your Highnesses the truth when I say that God has worked a miracle in him, for I have never seen a man so temperate in eating and drinking, outside of Spain. Indeed, such a thing seems to be superhuman in these countries. He lends a willing ear to his counsellors, and decides nothing without asking them; but in greater matters he acts according to his own judgement, and in my opinion, he generally makes a right decision. I recognize him perfectly in this last peace, which was made against the wishes of the majority of his kingdom.

Tragically for Scotland, James made one fatal wrong decision. Provoked by his brother-in-law Henry VIII, newly succeeded to the throne of England, and out of a mistaken sense of chivalry towards Queen Anne of Brittany, he launched an invasion into England in the summer of 1513. Not many miles south of the Tweed he met an army under the Earl of Surrey. The place was called Flodden, and the tragic results of the battle are infamous. The appalling Scottish losses decimated a generation, and James himself was killed.

Scotland never really recovered. With James IV, the beloved, popular king, the greatest by far of all the house of Stewart, died the nobles who followed his standard in war and his civilizing influence in peace. With him also died many of those Latin-literate eldest sons (including his own brilliant young bastard son, the Archbishop of St Andrews), and the commoners who had rallied to his cause in their thousands because of their love and respect for him. And again the country was to suffer the uncertainties of a long minority: King James V was seventeen months old.

The involved and troubled politics of the minority years of Mary's father need not be pursued in detail here, but the predominant factors should be explained briefly. First and

ABOVE LEFT *James IV, Scotland's great Renaissance king. His death at Flodden in 1513, along with many of the leaders of his generation, was a blow from which the nation never really recovered.*

ABOVE *Mary's father, James V. After a minority during which his person was fought over by opposing factions, his period of personal rule lasted for sixteen years.*

foremost there was the Douglas family, as always on the look-out for family advancement through the control of an infant monarch. The old Earl of Angus had died at Flodden within the year. In the same year his grandson and heir had married Queen Margaret and thus acquired for himself the handy position of stepfather to the little king and his brother, the Duke of Ross, born after his father's death and destined to only a few years of life. James IV's will had appointed Queen Margaret as regent; but under its conditions, on her remarriage she forfeited this power to the 'second person' – the next adult male in line to the succession. Such a condition did not of course put paid to Angus's ambitions or to Margaret's, and the situation was further complicated by the disintegration of the marriage, which put the former partners into opposite political camps.

The 'second person' was virtually a Frenchman: John Stewart, Duke of Albany, half French by birth, French-speaking and married to a Frenchwoman. He was summoned by the Scots Parliament to leave his properties and friends in France. His reluctance to do this was quite understandable, and his honour in overcoming this reluctance and in trying to put some order into the power vacuum that was post-Flodden Scotland, while less comprehensible, was wholly creditable. Until 1524 he tried manfully to wrestle with the warring factions amongst the nobles and with the maverick and rather limited dowager; but it became too much for him and he returned to France, remaining a good friend to Scotland at the French court until his line died out with him in 1540.

James V was thus left to the mercy of the Douglases. His official 'coming of age' at fourteen made no difference to his position. An attempt to rescue him from their clutches while he was on a progress to the Borders ended in failure, and began a bitter blood feud between two of the most powerful families there, the Scotts and the Kerrs, which was to last for over a quarter of a century.

It was not until five years after Albany's departure that James escaped from the power of the Douglases, literally as well as figuratively. A careful plan to deceive his guards was set in motion, and early on a May morning in 1528 James, disguised as a groom, slipped away from Falkland and towards Stirling Castle, freedom, kingship – and revenge on the Douglases.

The teenager had acquired power at almost the same age as his father, but he was not of the same calibre. It is true that he had many positive qualities, but his formative parent was not the golden Stewart king he never remembered, but his mother, who had most of the Tudors' less admirable characteristics. But he had had as tutor one of the finest minds in Scotland: Sir David Lyndsay, poet and man of letters, author of *Ane Satyre of the Thrie Estaits*. James was himself a poet and, as we shall see in exploring many of the places associated with his daughter, was intensely interested in the architecture and the improvement of his palaces. But as in the heyday of Mary's reign, there was a certain superficiality about the court. This may have reflected the personality of its leader, or it may simply have been inevitable. The rising sun of Scottish Renaissance life had died in the slaughter at Flodden: the roots of new growths were shallow, and the storms around them too fierce to allow them to flourish.

He faced many of the same problems that had confronted his father, chief among them being the establishment of some kind of rule of law in the Highlands and Borders. He began with the Borders, mounting two ferociously punitive expeditions. His execution of two of the most notorious of the Border freebooters, John Armstrong of Gilnockie and Perys Cockburn of Henderland, have been immortalized in two of the finest anonymous Border ballads, 'Johnnie Armstrong' and 'The Border Widow's Lament'. They are desperately subjective, of course, but they are an indication of how James came to be regarded by the people of the Borders, his first line of defence against the 'auld enemy':

> To seek hot water beneath cauld ice
> It surely is a great folly;
> I have asked grace from a graceless face,
> But there is none for my men and me.

Nor did the newly potent king refrain from imprisoning those Border earls and lairds whom he perceived as too sympathetic to the wild men they lived amongst. Even those who had supported his bids for freedom, such as Bothwell, Maxwell, Home and Buccleuch, served terms of imprisonment.

His progress to the Highlands was a much more douce affair: perhaps the enthusiasm with which he had tackled the troublesome Borderers had a salutary effect on the Highlanders. And if there was poverty beyond the Highland line, there was wealth too: a description of the accommodation and entertainment provided for the king and his mother by the Earl of Atholl indicates the standard of living enjoyed by those at the top of the social order: 'A rustic palace built in a fair meadow, of green timber woven about with birches . . . a great round tower at each corner . . . a moat, a drawbridge,' with the turf floor 'strewn with rushes, meadowsweet and flowers . . . well roofed and hung within with fine tapestries and silken arrases, and set with fine glass windows on all sides.' For drink the royal party was supplied with ale, beer, white wine, claret, malmsey, muscatel, alicante, hippocras and aqua vitae. Food included almond bread and gingerbread, beef, mutton, lamb, rabbit, crane, swan, goose, partridge and plover, duck, turkey, peacock, blackcock, moorfowl and capercailzie.

One of James's most attractive characteristics, about which we shall learn more in looking at royal Fife, was that he was willing to discard such finery and comfort. He would frequently dress in casual, simple attire, and move undiscovered amongst his subjects: a stratagem which his daughter also employed, more infrequently and less successfully. But however he might enjoy the simple life, and however much he might take part in the country revels he describes so well in his poem 'Christis Kirke on the Greene', he was still king. He might pursue and seduce country girls or the daughters of his earls and lairds, he might and did seriously love one woman: but the King of Scots had high merchandising power on the international marriage market. And financial and political needs would force him to transact a suitable contract.

Both his marriages were to French princesses (Mary of Guise was raised to the rank of 'daughter of France' for her marriage), stating clearly the bias of Scottish foreign policy towards the old ally, France. The chief architect of this policy from now on was Cardinal David Beaton, Archbishop of St Andrews. Beaton, however, was less a theologian than a politician, and a highly skilled one at that. But he was ultimately a bad adviser to the king: his influence in holding back reform of the church from within, and his refusal to deal with abuses and injustices which had grown up under the system to which he adhered, ultimately undermined not only James's authority over his lords, but also the Catholic church as an institution in Scotland, and the alliance with France.

But that was far ahead. James had been contracted to marry the French king's daughter under the Treaty of Rouen in 1521, when he was only eight. The wedding finally came about in 1537, when he married Francis I's daughter Madeleine, a frail and pretty girl of sixteen. The marriage caught the public imagination, and their return to Scotland after the splendid marriage in France was greeted with great enthusiasm. Madeleine, on her part, gracefully kissed the Scottish soil on landing. Within six weeks she was beneath it: all parties feared her lifespan would be brief, and the air of Balmerino Abbey, which her husband considered 'the best in Scotland' could neither contain nor cure what appears to have been tuberculosis.

Mary of Guise had been married to the Duke of Vendôme, and was widowed at about the same time as James. It was a political marriage for both (on Madeleine's side, at any rate, the first French marriage had been a love match). Another newly widowed king entered the lists for the hand of the Duchess of Vendôme, James's uncle, Henry VIII. The story is often related that he declared that he was 'big in person and needed a big wife', to which the canny Mary replied that though her stature was large, her neck was little. She was the eldest of a large family: all rich, powerful, intensely capable – and highly ambitious. With her marriage to James the influence of the Guise family became an important factor in Scottish politics, and it continued to be so after his death. Mary, the only surviving child of this union, would form another link with the royal house of Valois, and through her the Guise family would reach the pinnacle of their power.

# 2

# THE BIRTHPLACE:
# LINLITHGOW

*E*ven today Linlithgow Palace, in its roofless grandeur, seems to the visitor a fitting birthplace for a queen. Walk through the archway of its outer entrance, decorated with carved panels of the four orders of chivalry to which James v belonged, and you seem to step back into the sixteenth century. For although time and fire have destroyed, later centuries have added little. The ornate fountain in the centre of the castle's quadrangle, which owes more to continental Europe than to Scotland, symbolizes the kind of court which both James IV and James v tried to create.

The palace is flanked on one side by Linlithgow Loch and on the other by the ancient parish church of St Michael. Set above the busy twentieth-century dormitory town, it creates a skyline basically unchanged since the late autumn of 1542, when Mary of Guise made her way through that same courtyard to await her fourth confinement. She had borne two sons to James v in rapid succession after their marriage, and both had died within a month of each other, almost exactly a year previously. She had had to leave her only surviving child, the son of her first husband, in France when she had married James.

James, for his part, already had at least seven living children by five known mothers. Elizabeth Shaw of Sauchie, Elizabeth Beaton of Creich, Elizabeth Stewart (he showed some consistency) and Euphemia Carmichael all subsequently returned to historical obscurity. But Margaret Erskine, mother of Lord James Stewart, reappears later in the travels of Mary Stuart as the mother also of her jailer on Lochleven.

James v had been born at Linlithgow, and it appears to have been the favourite residence of Mary of Guise. In her superbly diplomatic way she praised it as the most princely palace she had ever seen – a touch of hyperbole, perhaps, from one brought up amongst the lavishness of the French châteaux, but an acknowledgment that Linlithgow, of all Scottish royal residences, could stand comparison with the buildings of her own land. Certainly over the century that preceded her arrival it had received consistent attentions from its royal trustees.

Linlithgow had boasted a manor house which was part of the royal circuit as early as the reign of David I in the twelfth century, but the first monarch with whom it is closely associated was the mighty King Edward I or England, '*Malleum Scotorum*' (Hammer of the Scots). At the beginning of the fourteenth century, during his campaign to conquer and annex Scotland, he turned the existing manor house into a defensive structure to house a convenient garrison of occupying soldiers. Later he used it as a strategic base for the siege of Stirling Castle. It seems to have been an assembly point for ballistic siege-engines, some of which were built in Linlithgow and some of which, amazingly, were transported by sea from Dunfermline, where Edward had made his winter headquarters.

By 1305 Edward appeared to have subjugated Scotland completely, but within eight years resistance to English rule was victorious under the leadership of Robert the Bruce, the hero-king and soldier who waged a skilful campaign of guerrilla warfare. Today we would

IACOBVS.QVINTVS.SCOTTORVM.REX ℣ ANNO.ÆTATIS.SVE. Z 8

MARIA.LOTHORINGIA.ILLIVS.IN.SECVNDIS.NVPTIIS VXOR·ℓANNO ÆTATIS SVE. Z 4 ℣

LEFT *After the death of Queen Madeleine, James married another French wife, the widowed Mary of Guise.*

OPPOSITE *Across the loch, the skyline of palace and church dominate the town of Linlithgow.*

call it terrorism. Apart from Sir William Wallace, who had led the resistance until his execution in 1305, the names of the main leaders of the struggle came from other noble families: the good Sir James Douglas (or the Black Douglas, so called, we are told, for his complexion and not his deeds) and Sir Thomas Randolph. But there were humbler heroes too. One of them was William Bunnock, a Linlithgow farmer whose hay was requisitioned by the English garrison. Bunnock concocted an ingenious and risky plan to capture the peel for Bruce. A party of armed men was hidden in a consignment of hay, while others took up concealed positions in the vicinity of the tower: as the haycart passed through the gateway, Bunnock cut loose the horse, leaving the cart in the entry so that the portcullis could not be lowered. The guard was overpowered, the tower captured, and its inhabitants massacred either by Bunnock's men or by the country people with whom they sought refuge. In due course the enterprising farmer was rewarded by Bruce with a grant of land.

After Bruce dismantled its fortifications in 1310, Linlithgow's role as a defensive structure disappeared. It continued to be used sporadically as a royal manor house throughout the fourteenth and early fifteenth centuries, until a fire in 1424 left James I with a prime site on which to develop the kind of palace with which he must have become familiar during his long years in England.

In 1406 King Robert III had sent his eleven-year-old son James to France for his own protection. Ironically, the ship the child sailed in was captured by pirates, and the young prince was sent as a prisoner to the court of the English king, Henry IV. Within weeks Robert III died, and King James I of Scotland remained captive for the next eighteen years – for the rest of Henry IV's reign, throughout the reign of Henry V and into the reign of Henry VI. The year of the fire at Linlithgow marked the end of the king's captivity, which had been of a most privileged kind. Hostages of noble or regal rank were kept in surroundings appropriate to their status, but they were prisoners none the less. James's long poem, *The King's Quair*, written in the last year of his imprisonment, begins with a cry for freedom:

Whereas in ward full oft would I bewail
My deadly life, full of pain and penance,
Saying right thus, 'What guilt have I, to fail
My freedom in this world and my pleasance?'
Since every man has thereof sufficience,
That I behold; and I a creature
Put from all this – hard is mine adventure.
The bird, the beast, the fish eke in the sea,
They live in freedom each one with his kind;
And I a man and liketh liberty;
What shall I say, what reason shall I find,
That fortune should do so? Thus in my mind
My folk I would argue, but all in vain,
None there was took pity on my pain.

There were conditions to his release, one of which was that he should marry an English subject. It was a condition he found only too pleasurable to fulfil: in the gardens of one of his places of captivity he had seen and fallen in love with Lady Joan Beaufort, the 'milk-white dove', a granddaughter of the great John of Gaunt. Later in *The King's Quair*, he describes his first sight of her:

In her was youth, beauty with humble port,
Bounty, richness, and womanly feature,
God better knows than can my pen report,
Wisdom, largesse, estate and knowledge sure.
In every point, so goodly her measure
In word, in deed, in shape, in countenance,
That nature might no more her child advance.

Such was his tribute to her in words; Linlithgow Palace might well have been his architectural poem. There is no doubt that both of them took a keen interest in its building: in the early stages, King James lodged with a 'goodwife' in the town to supervise operations, and he seems to have taken up residence as soon as the building was habitable. Over £4,500 was put towards Linlithgow Palace: tiles were imported from Flanders, and the king's painter was put in charge of the decorative details. On the eastern wall of the palace, high on what was the side wall of the grand hall, is an unusual window with fourteen small apertures which, it is thought, illuminated a richly painted ceiling. The number of times that the royal couple stayed there indicates that it was probably their favourite residence; and though it is well placed strategically, it was built by James as befitted a peace-time palace, in a kingdom where his ambition 'that the key should keep the castle, and the bracken bush the cow' had been achieved.

Two generations passed before such royal favour beamed on Linlithgow Palace again. Then it became a focus for the activities, architectural and cultural, of Scotland's Renaissance kings, James IV and James V. The former added galleries, stairs and passages: in his youth he had visited northern Italy, and he was no doubt influenced by the buildings there. Certainly, the long galleries on the east and south sides of the palace have an Italianate air to them. It was at Linlithgow that his son was born, and there that Queen Margaret waited after he set out on the ill-starred Flodden campaign of 1513. His departure from Linlithgow was not without incident: but that episode belongs in the story of the neighbouring St Michael's church.

ABOVE *The courtyard of Linlithgow Palace, birthplace of Mary Queen of Scots, and the ornate fountain erected by her father.*

OPPOSITE *Sir David Lyndsay of the Mount, poet and tutor to James V. His great dramatic masterpiece,* Ane Satyre of the Thrie Estaits, *was first performed in Linlithgow Palace.*

James v, though harassed by pressure from his uncle, Henry viii, and perpetually on call to deal with domestic unrest, nevertheless managed during the thirteen years of his personal rule to establish a flourishing court life. His birthplace benefited: some of his adornments have already been referred to – the carved panel above the new entrance he created on the south rather than the east side of the palace, and the ornate fountain with its nude musicians and its heraldic tribute to James and both his French wives. If Falkland Palace in Fife was the centre of his private enjoyments, Linlithgow was the scene of his splendid public life. A vast army of staff was employed to see to the comforts of the court, and the banquets in the great hall were magnificent both in their gastronomic offerings – domestic and imported produce including such delicacies as goose, swan, peacock, sturgeon and porpoise – and in their entertainment. Musicians from Scotland and Europe played, and poets declaimed (James v, like his great-grandfather, was the author of some respectable poetry, and even arranged a 'flyting', or competition, between himself and brother poets). Linlithgow was also the setting for the first performance of Sir David Lyndsay's great dramatic work *Ane Satyre of the Thrie Estaits*, a warning to the king of the dangers of pleasure-seeking, and a political statement of the aims of those who wished to reform the church from within. In view of the play's outspokenness, not to mention its length (five hours), it seems surprising that the king sanctioned a repeat performance. But such early promise faded and the closing years of his reign were marked by increasingly repressive legislation with regard to religious freedom and reform, so that those who pressed for the latter were increasingly thrown into the anti-French, pro-English lobby.

By the autumn of 1542, James v was losing the support not only of the clergy but also of a considerable number of his nobles, and it was at this inauspicious time that he was obliged to muster against Henry viii. His forces were half-hearted and under strength, and the foray itself was as misconceived as had been the Flodden campaign. Nevertheless the Scots outnumbered the English force at Solway Moss on 24 November, and their ignominious defeat can be attributed largely to low morale and the poor generalship of the king's favourite, Oliver Sinclair, whose appointment had further alienated the already disaffected troops.

In the grip of a depressive illness which now became acute, James visited his pregnant queen at Linlithgow, but did not stay for the birth. Perhaps the memory of the two dead princes was more than his rather facile nature could bear. His lack of interest in their replacement, as in everything, has been attributed solely to his state of mental collapse following the disgrace of Solway Moss. Perhaps it stretches twentieth-century credibility too far to suggest that a hitherto healthy thirty-one-year-old man should die of melancholia in three weeks, and it is a more likely hypothesis that there was a physical cause for his sudden collapse and death. He withdrew to his beloved Falkland Palace where, after the news of his daughter's birth had been brought to him, in the well-known description of the chronicler Pitscottie, 'He turned him upon his back, and looked up and beheld all his nobles and lords about him, and gave up a little smile of laughter, and thereafter held up his hands to God and yielded up his spirit.'

At Linlithgow, his widow was faced with the manifold tasks of motherhood and politics, the primary concern in each area being the health and safety of the little queen. James, second Earl of Arran, who assumed the regency, could not be regarded as a disinterested party as he was next in line to the throne. Arran's affiliation for the immediate present with the pro-English party, the general civil unrest and the predatoriness of Henry viii, Mary's one-time rejected suitor and uncle by marriage, made Linlithgow an increasingly unsuitable residence. It could house a court, but not a militia. When the baby was seven months old Mary of Guise removed her to the secure fortress of Stirling Castle.

During Mary Stuart's personal reign she seems to have had little affection for her birthplace. The splendours of her court were all centred on Holyrood, and her journeyings in the rest of her kingdom were marked by simplicity rather than grandeur. Linlithgow, which of all the Scottish royal houses came nearest to the scale to which she had become accustomed in France, merely served its turn as a stopover for journeys to the west.

In her son's reign it regained some of its favour, though the glittering opulence of the early part of the century was eclipsed by the austerity of post-Reformation Scotland. But he summoned the Estates there in 1585, in spite of having been warned that the west quarter was becoming unsafe. Ten years later, with James sitting on the throne in London, he was warned that a collapse of the north side could happen at any time. Two years later it did, and between 1618 and 1620 major restoration work was carried out.

Thereafter decay continued and visits by royalty became infrequent. Charles I stayed there in the seventeenth century, as did Bonnie Prince Charlie in the following century: it was during the Jacobite Rebellion headed by him that accidental fires put the last touches to the ravages of the palace. Only the conservation-conscious twentieth century has tried to make amends, and the citizens of today's dormitory town make every effort to bring life and laughter back to its walls, staging colourful festivals with attractions including such age-old pastimes as jousting.

Although the palace boasted a chapel, this was used for private devotions only. Royalty and their entourage worshipped frequently at St Michael's parish church next door, and its beauty and pre-eminence were the results of this attention. It was the setting for Mary's baptism, though unlike that of her son – about which more can be read in the following chapter – this was such a low-key affair as to remain without documentation. However, the placing of the ceremony in St Michael's is undisputed.

St Michael's pre-dates the palace, but time and care have served it better. The earliest mention of a church on that site is – almost predictably – in the reign of the saintly King David I, who gifted it, in 1138, to the cathedral church of St Andrews. But the wording of his charter indicates that there had been a church foundation here for some centuries. St Michael's was dedicated in 1242, and parts at least of the present building seem to date from before the Wars of Independence. The proximity of the church to Edward's peel tower led to its enclosure within the fortifications, where it was used not as a house of prayer but as a weaponry and fodder store, referred to in contemporary English documents as 'the great church'. So much for Edward's sensibilities towards the institutions of the people he hoped to rule.

A fire in the roof of the nave is recorded in 1424; it seems likely that this was caused by the same fire that destroyed the palace that year. Such damage as there was had been made good by the time the royal couple attended worship there five years later. Throughout the fifteenth century funds poured in for the building and its embellishment: from the royal coffers, from the citizens of Linlithgow, from customs duties and from fines (levied partly from those careless residents of the town who allowed their chimneys to blaze out of control – an early measure of pollution control).

The nave and chancel were completed in the late fifteenth century, in the reign of James IV. It was in connection with him that the most famous episode in the history of St Michael's took place. The king was spending the last few days before the expedition of 1513 with his wife (another permanent farewell to another pregnant queen, as it turned out) and his infant son. Before setting out he attended evening devotions, presumably to pray for the success of his venture. From the shadows there stepped a wraith-like form, who addressed him in warning tones. Sir Walter Scott, in his epic poem on Flodden, *Marmion*, sets the scene:

*St Michael's church has a long and interesting history, one episode of which was the baptism of Queen Mary.*

In Katharine's aisle the monarch knelt,
With sack-cloth shirt, and iron belt,
   And eyes with sorrow streaming;
Around him in their stalls of state,
The Thistle's knight-companions sate,
   Their banners o'er them beaming.

Stepped from the crowd a ghostly wight,
In azure gown, with cincture white;
His forehead bald, his head was bare,
Down hung at length his yellow hair.

He stepped before the Monarch's chair,
And stood with rustic plainness there,
   And little reverence made;
Not head, nor body, bow'd nor bent,
But on the desk his arm he leant,
   And words like these he said
In a low voice, but never tone
So thrilled through nerve, and vein, and bone:
'My mother sent me from afar,
Sir King, to warn thee not to war,
   Woe waits on thine array.'

The Assassination of Regent Moray. *In 1570 Mary's brother, and rival for power, was gunned down in the main street of Linlithgow.*

   The rest of his message was concerned with warning the king against the dangers of extra-marital associations. The queen was suspected of having engineered the apparition, and James, tragically, was undeterred.

   St Michael's as it is today was finally completed in the heyday of his son's reign with the addition of the apse. This event was celebrated in 1531 by the granting of a royal charter to the burgh of Linlithgow. Like the towns of the Borders, Linlithgow carries out one of the conditions of that charter to this day, when once a year its citizens undertake an inspection of the marches, or boundaries. Here, however, the inspection takes place on foot, unlike in the Border burghs, where hundreds of horsemen make a dramatic sight.

   The building in which Mary was baptized thus remains structurally the same, though differently adorned. Then, twenty niches above the buttresses contained the images of a variety of saints; now only St Michael himself remains, sole survivor of the systematic 'cleansing' of the church by John Knox and his followers in 1559. Swept away, too, were the twenty-four altars within the church.

For over three centuries St Michael's was used for a variety of purposes besides that of worship: as a timber store, as classrooms for Edinburgh University during the plague of the mid-seventeenth century, and as a stable and dormitory for Cromwell's soldiers. Galleries were built and removed (during the time when half the church was in use with galleries Robert Burns observed on a visit, 'what a miserable thing, is Presbyterian worship!') and in the early part of the eighteenth century the original stone crown surmounting the tower was removed for safety reasons. When in the 1960s the time came to complete the massive task of stonework restoration with the replacement of the crown, a problem was apparent: no two artists' impressions gave a similar interpretation of the original structure. It was thus decided to create a form in the best of the new traditions rather than attempt to imitate the uncertain past, and the result is the striking and graceful crown of thorns by the sculptor Geoffrey Clarke, who had worked on the new Coventry Cathedral. Restoration work had begun in 1894, and continues today, with the dedication in September 1986 of a small side chapel in the south aisle. Throughout this century artists and craftsmen, supported by the residents of the prosperous modern town, have produced as true a renascence of St Michael's as did those of the times of Mary Stuart's father and grandfather; and today's infants are baptized in surroundings no less celebratory of the majesty of God.

There is one last link between the town of Linlithgow and the life – though not the reign – of Mary Stuart. It was here, on 23 January 1570, that her once-loved and later discredited half-brother, the Earl of Moray, who became regent when she was forced to abdicate in 1567, was assassinated. He died at the hands of one James Hamilton of Bothwellhaugh, whose motive appears to have been twofold: he bore a mainly personal grudge, but he was also undoubtedly part of a wider conspiracy.

James Stewart, created Earl of Moray by Mary eight years before his death, was one of the principal actors in the pageant of her years in Scotland. More than that, he was the major and most capable politician of his day, whose firmly held convictions pointed Scotland towards the peaceful inheritance of the English crown. He was not a charismatic figure (he receives unsympathetic treatment in novels about the period) but he was an extremely effective bastard of the royal variety. With hindsight we may regret the success of his policies, but it has to be admitted that they were the result of genuine conviction, not personal self-seeking.

James Stewart was born in 1533, the product of James v's most serious premarital liaison. If Margaret, daughter of Lord Erskine, had been unmarried, James might well have reverted to the early Stewart kings' practice of marrying a well-born subject rather than a foreign princess. Even so, the relationship was such that three years after James Stewart's birth, a divorce was under consideration between Margaret and her husband, Robert Douglas of Lochleven. This came to nothing; but King James was solicitous for the welfare of his bastards, and in 1538 he secured the future of his five-year-old son by endowing him with the lucrative post of Commendator of St Andrews. It was appointments such as this, debasing positions within the church and abusing the power they commanded, that bred dissension and disaffection among priests and laymen alike.

Even James Stewart himself, originally a staunch supporter of Mary of Guise, became at the age of twenty-five a convert to John Knox's form of Protestantism. He was indeed a prime prize for the revolutionaries in the struggle ahead for the soul of Scotland. Initially he remained on good terms with Mary of Guise, but eventually political considerations outweighed personal scruples. General resentment of abuses within the Catholic church was fanned by indignation at the presence in Scotland of a French army of occupation, used by

Mary of Guise (acting as regent while her young daughter was educated at the French court) as a tool for administration and, in Scottish eyes at least, for domination. Mary of Guise became identified with the Catholic party within the country, and popular distrust of both the French and Catholicism combined to swell the ranks of the Protestant cause, whose members called themselves the 'Congregation of the Lord'. Under the leadership of its prophet, John Knox, the combination became explosive, and in 1559 it erupted in the form of a religious revolution, led by nobles styled the 'Lords of the Congregation'. Moray was among their number, and he became joint inheritor of the queen regent's powers when the lords toppled her from power later that year, just before her death.

By the time of Mary's return to Scotland in 1561, Moray had emerged as the leading political figure in the country. Moreover, he was acceptable to the new regime in England. He enjoyed a close rapport with Elizabeth: not only were they alike in strength, capability, and deviousness, but it is also not beyond the bounds of probability that she, so often branded with bastardy, would have had some sympathy with James's status. He would have made so much better a sovereign than Mary, yet he had to be content with the masterminding of policy through her. In 1561, having just established his authority, he must have felt the death of her husband Francis II and her return to Scotland as a blow to the continuity of his policies. He must indeed have hoped that one of the foreign marriages projected for her would be achieved. Nevertheless, he behaved towards her with great correctness and even affection: it was not until she first acquired Rizzio as a confidant and then married Darnley that he defied her, and broke the relationship that he had carefully nurtured over the years. Having originally supported Darnley's suit, he quickly became aware not only of the unsuitability of that young man's character – obvious to everyone in the young queen's court except herself – but also the threat that he posed to Mary's power and ambition.

He was banished after his unsuccessful rebellion on the occasion of that marriage, only to return at the time of Rizzio's murder, in which he was undoubtedly implicated. Never again did he enjoy the complete trust of his half-sister, though it was soon obvious that his assessment of Darnley was only too accurate. But she was never capable of acting without strong male support during her reign, and now she turned increasingly and fatally to Bothwell. When her marriage to the latter led her inexorably towards deposition and imprisonment, Moray's hour came. He was elected regent of the infant James VI, and after defeating Mary at the battle of Langside in 1568 became undisputed ruler of Scotland.

But it was in that battle that the seeds of his own destruction were sown: for Hamilton of Bothwellhaugh fought for the queen, and had his property confiscated as a result. Worse than that, his wife, according to a contemporary source, 'not thinking to be punished for her husband's fact, set down in her own house, where she intended simply ... to have remained'. But she was driven out, 'all her goods taken from her, and she left stark naked'. She was allegedly driven mad by this experience, which was the genesis of Bothwellhaugh's revenge.

The murder of Moray robbed Scotland of its most skilful politician. His hand would have been a more reliable and honourable one to guide the affairs of his nephew James VI than that of the child's paternal grandfather, Regent Lennox. And, twenty years on, intervention by him with Elizabeth would surely have saved Mary's head.

Moray's influence on the direction Scotland took in the mid-sixteenth century was infinitely more lasting and definitive than that of his half-sister, the lawfully anointed queen. The course on which the nation was set – towards an acceptable inheritance by the Scots monarch of the English throne – owed as much to the political foundation he had laid for such an event as to the lack of fertility of the house of Tudor.

*James Stewart, Earl of Moray, by Hans Eworth, 1561. The eldest of James v's children, Moray had every quality needed to make a great king, except one – legitimacy.*

# 3

## THE NURSERY: STIRLING

*Stirling Castle, where Mary spent the years of her infancy, secure from the attentions of her great uncle Henry VIII and his 'rough wooing'.*

Almost all of the Scottish part of Mary's childhood was spent in the safety of Stirling Castle. Like Edinburgh and Dumbarton, Stirling has always been one of the great fortresses on which the safety of the kingdom depended. The precipitous rock rising from the level plain of the Forth valley has assured the castle not only the most awe-inspiring panoramas in Scotland, but also its central role in the troubled history of the country. Aptly named the 'Gateway to the Highlands', it straddles the natural road from the Highlands to the Lowlands and guards what for centuries was the only bridge over the mighty River Forth. Until recent times there were no ferries below Stirling, and the fords above it, where they existed, were in mountainous and difficult country. Together with Dumbarton, Stirling holds the line of country between the Forth and the Clyde, and therefore both the north-south and east-west routes across the country could be defended from this fortress.

The ancient name for Stirling, 'Stryvelin', meaning 'strife', is taken to denote the meeting of the three rivers, the Forth, Teith and Allan, to the east of the castle. The more modern form is derived from 'ster' meaning a mountain, and 'lin' meaning a river, which exactly describes its position.

Stirling was one of the castles yielded to Henry II of England as part of the ransom for the return of William the Lion in 1174, and was later bought back from Henry's successor Richard I. In the following century, the most effective method of securing power in Scotland was put into practice by the Earls of Menteith and Buchan, who seized the sixteen-year-old King Alexander III and the great royal seal and carried both off to Stirling Castle. Alexander III died in 1286, leaving no direct heir to the throne, when his horse stumbled over a cliff top; his widow, Queen Yoletta, however, was reported to be with child. She stayed on at Stirling to make preparations for the birth for nearly a year before the mistake was finally discovered and she was shamefully escorted out of Scotland.

Five years later Scotland was under the guardianship of Edward I of England, and all castles were delivered into English hands. The ferocious Wars of Independence followed, and the Scots regained control of Stirling. But 1296 found Edward again on the march from Linlithgow, laying waste and casting such fear before him that when he arrived in Stirling the fortress was deserted, with the keys nailed to the door. Edward claimed overlordship of Scotland and subjected the land to direct rule by English nobles and troops.

The following year William Wallace, a guerrilla leader of genius, led the Scots to their famous victory over the English at Stirling Bridge. The Scottish nobles failed to hold on to the 'Gateway to the Highlands', however, regaining it only in 1299, after besieging the castle until the ninety unfortunate defenders were reduced to eating three grey mares 'for default of other food'. By 1305 the English were again in possession of the fortress, flaunting their dominance along with one quarter of the body of Sir William Wallace, which they put on view on the castle walls.

The Scottish revenge came in 1314, under Robert the Bruce, with the resounding victory at Bannockburn. The king's brother, Edward Bruce, had been laying siege to the stronghold for approaching a year when Edward II brought an immense army to its relief. In the battle that ensued Robert the Bruce inflicted a crushing defeat on the English, after which he had the castle and towers levelled to the ground to prevent them ever being reheld against the Scots. It was to no avail, however, for by 1335 Edward III had taken residence, restored the fortifications and installed a garrison of nearly two hundred English soldiers. But now English military aggression was diverted towards France, in a war which was to continue sporadically for over a hundred years. Seven years after Edward had installed himself there, Stirling was surrendered without bloodshed under siege to Robert Stewart, the guardian, when war in France meant that no relief for the English was forthcoming.

After such stormy times the castle then enjoyed a relatively peaceful period which lasted until the beginning of the fifteenth century, when under the Stewarts it again rose to prominence as the scene of some of the gayest, and also the bloodiest, episodes in Scottish history. One of the most notorious misdeeds was the murder of the Earl of Douglas by the Scottish King James II in 1452. Under suspicion of plotting against the throne, the 'Black Earl' was summoned to Stirling for an audience, with the king's sworn oath that he would have safe conduct. But on the evening of his arrival the king's volatile temper was so aroused that he seized a dagger and plunged it into Douglas's neck, then fell upon him with the other lords, and finally pushed the bloody corpse out of the window. The site of this brutal murder, the memory of which was to dog the Stewarts throughout their reign, is still referred to as the 'Douglas Room'.

Stirling nevertheless became the favourite residence of the Stewarts, but it was not until the reign of James IV that the building of the great hall and the magnificent Renaissance palace, and the rebuilding of the chapel royal were undertaken. He went daily to the chapel royal and there repented of his part in his father's death (James III was murdered after being defeated in battle by rebel lords with the young James IV at their head), causing an iron girdle to be made which he wore for the rest of his life, every year adding an ounce to its weight. Court life at Stirling was now one of revelry, entertainment and experiment, the days filled with hawking, hunting, jousting and walking in the pleasure gardens beneath the castle walls. French and Italian craftsmen gathered there, painting, carving and plastering the new buildings, and the scientists of the day took advantage of generous royal patronage. One such Italian monk invited the court to witness his triumph over gravity, boldly flinging himself from a parapet with artificial wings strapped to his back. He was fortunate to escape with a broken thigh.

After James IV's death at the battle of Flodden the new baby king, James V, was brought to Stirling, where he was to spend much of his life. As a child he amused himself chasing the white peacocks around the fishponds and flowerbeds of the gardens, skirting around the lions' house in the courtyard, or sneaking out of the castle (a habit he was to carry with him into later life) to 'Hurly Haaky' Hill', so called because of his pastime of coasting down its steep slope on a cow's skull ('haaky' meaning cow).

In 1536 James V left Stirling for France to fetch home his French bride. Two years later Mary Stuart's mother, Queen Mary of Guise, arrived at Stirling. In August of 1543 the infant Queen Mary was brought here for safety from her birthplace at Linlithgow, and the following month, like her father, she was crowned in the chapel royal, with, as was reported to Henry VIII, 'such solemnity as they use in this country, which is not very costly'. Only two days after the unceremonious coronation, Henry urged the seizure of the castle and its tiny royal inmate, and only the massive fortifications of the castle dissuaded the treacherous Scottish lords from the attempt.

Two views of the peaceful priory on the island of Inchmahome in the Lake of Menteith, where Mary was taken for greater safety after the Scottish defeat at Pinkie Cleugh.

So jealously guarded at Stirling was the young queen that 'no noble in the realm might enter the castle with more than two servants in the company', and only the queen dowager had free access to her daughter. In 1545 the Privy Council put the sole care of Mary at Stirling into the hands of Lords Erskine and Livingstone, for the costly sum of £60 a month. Mary spent the first five years of her life in Scotland, and during that time Henry carried out a vicious and relentless campaign of persecution against the Scots, known as the 'rough wooing'. Even after his death the harassment continued. In 1547 Somerset, protector of the young Edward VI, mounted an expedition which culminated at the battle of Pinkie Cleugh in September, when the Scots were routed. By now, rival claims on the royal infant had reached a pitch where her safety could no longer be guaranteed, and she was stealthily removed by her mother to the priory on the island of Inchmahome in the Lake of Menteith, in the care of the Commendator, John Erskine, later Earl of Mar.

The ruins of this Augustinian priory are today one of the most attractive memorials to monastic life left in Scotland. Mary stayed there in safety for less than three weeks, but so many parts of the little island are named after her that it is possible that she revisited this peaceful priory during her stays at Stirling Castle in later life.

It is interesting, incidentally, that the Lake of Menteith is alone in Scotland in *not* being a loch, but instead takes the English form of its name. The tradition is that this was because Sir William Wallace's betrayer, Sir John Menteith, owned the surrounding area. There is no truth whatever in this – the lake and its countryside were the properties of the *earls* of Menteith, who had no part in Wallace's capture, so it requires another explanation.

In September 1561, on her return to Scotland from France as reigning queen, Mary returned to Stirling Castle during her first triumphant progress through her kingdom, but her two-day stay proved almost fatal. A burning candle in her chamber set fire to her curtains and bed while she was asleep, and she was discovered smothering in the smoke.

Four years later, it was here that she personally nursed the sick Lord Darnley through illness. During this tender and intimate period of close proximity she became besotted with him. A twenty-four-year-old widow – and probably a virginal one at that – baulked of a glittering second foreign marriage that had for so long been negotiated, closeted with a handsome youth fresh from the graceful and glorious court of their mutual cousin Elizabeth, was almost bound to find the situation highly erotic. Couple that with the fact that Darnley *was* regarded as a potential suitor, that there *was* a telling dynastic argument (having both Tudor and Stewart blood he fortified her claim to the English throne) – and the match, for all Moray's sensible attempts to prevent it, was unstoppable. She could hardly have made a worse choice than this golden, weak, decadent young man, for he was to be her downfall.

By the time of the birth in June 1566 of the child of that union, the future king of both Scotland and England, she knew her mistake, and could count the cost in personal terms. The baby was taken to Stirling, the traditional nursery of Scottish princes, and here was christened in December of that year. The baptism was to be a show of splendour to foreign ambassadors, above all to those of her baby's godmother, Queen Elizabeth. Mary had originally hoped that the occasion would be lent even more significance by a visit in person from the godmother; in the event Mary's half-sister, the Countess of Argyll, stood proxy and the meeting of the two queens did not take place, then or ever.

Arrangements for the splendid occasion were in the hands of Bothwell, who had become Mary's most trusted adviser. He could not, however, alter the fact that the baptism was to be according to the Catholic faith, so, along with other Protestant lords, he did not actually enter the chapel for the ceremony. The only element of the Catholic rite that Mary decided to dispense with was the use of the episcopal spittle.

*Henry, Lord Darnley, and his younger brother Charles, painted by Hans Eworth in 1563. In 1565 Mary nursed Darnley through illness at Stirling Castle, and fell victim to the infatuation that was to change the course of her reign.*

THES BE THE SONES OF ℱ RIGHE HONERABLES FERLLE OF LENOXE AD TE LADY MARGARETZ GRACE, COVNTYES OF LENOXE AD ANGWYSE,

1563

CHARLLES STEWARDE HIS BROTHER, ÆTATIS, 6,    HENRY STEWARDE LORD DAR̄LEY AND DOWGLAS, ÆTATIS, 17,

All the trappings of the ceremony were sumptuous: the baptismal cloth of state was made of crimson velvet, edged with gold thread, crimson silk, and gold braid; the baby's bedspread took ten yards of figured cloth of silver; and the massive golden font – a present from Elizabeth – in workmanship and ornamentation 'combined elegance with value'. Conspicuous by his absence from the celebrations was the baby's father, who stayed in his quarters. But at least he was in the castle, which at one point he had threatened not to be: such a humiliation for Mary would also have raised doubts as to the prince's legitimacy.

By now, after only seventeen months of marriage, during which time he had given his spiteful and self-indulgent nature free rein, Mary's infatuation with Darnley was a thing of the past. His horrific murder of her secretary David Rizzio in March of that year set the seal on her loathing and contempt for him. She had been convinced that her life and that of her unborn child were equally at risk from Darnley and his ambition to become the sole ruler of Scotland, and now that she had her longed-for son and heir she was not going to let Darnley's sulks spoil the occasion of his christening. On the evening of the ceremony there was supper and dancing, music and comedy turns; next day the festivities continued with a bull hunt in the park, a banquet and a highly theatrical masque, and pyrotechnics. It was probably the most glorious spectacle that Stirling Castle ever saw.

Three months later, in March 1567, the now fatherless prince (Darnley himself having become the victim of another brutal murder) was given into the keeping of the Earl of Mar

RIGHT *A carving at Stirling Castle reputed to be a representation of James V.*

BELOW *The King's Knot, viewed from the ramparts of Stirling Castle.*

at Stirling Castle. Five weeks after that his mother rode to Stirling to visit him. They never met again. He was ten months old.

The French influence on the Scottish court was such that the buildings constructed at Stirling are of outstanding architectural importance. The palace within the castle walls has one of the earliest attempts at a classical façade in Britain, the French sculptors adorning it with statues and gargoyles in a mixture of Renaissance and Gothic styles. The figures along the east side represent deities and mythological characters. Those on the south are soldiers, while those on the north include Cleopatra and the asp, Mary Stuart, and her father James v disguised as a commoner. Adopting the name the 'Laird of Ballangleich' he was fond of slipping out of the castle to mingle with the people incognito or to undertake some errand of gallantry. The name came from a steep path leading up to a low sally port or gate in the inner wall used by the king on these occasions, which was known as the road of Ballangleich, meaning 'windy pass', a name still abundantly justified.

On the other side of the ramparts the initials M.R., Maria Regina, can be seen carved in the stone. The place is known as Queen Mary's look-out, as it was one of her favourite places for sitting out and taking the air. In the valley below lies the King's Park, where deer were bred and kept for royal hunts. At the east end were the royal gardens where, although the fruit trees and flower beds have disappeared, the terraces and mounds on which they stood are still clearly visible. In the centre of these paths and mounds rises an octagonal mound of some size, flat on top, known as the King's Knot. This is said to have been the scene of court festivities, and presumably was a place for knightly reunions, for it was called the Round Table as early as the time of Bannockburn.

At the time of its completion at the beginning of the sixteenth century the great hall was one of the most splendid in Europe. It was intended for great state occasions, as by that time the living quarters in the castle had been so developed that the traditional function of the medieval hall was no longer required. One of the last of these great occasions was the baptism of James vi's son, Prince Henry, in 1594, when the centrepiece of the festivities was a forty-foot-high model ship in the centre of the hall. The hall itself is now being restored to its former glory after its conversion and use as an army barracks up to 1964. The magnificent hammerbeam roof survives, but much of the interior stonework has yet to be restored. The ornamentation of the inner chambers of the palace can be guessed at from the imposing fireplaces and the 'Stirling Heads', carved medallions representing Scottish noblemen and rulers, which adorned the ceilings of the king's apartments.

The long shadow of Darnley continued to cast its shade over Stirling Castle even after his death. In 1571, four years after Mary's sad last visit to the castle, the Archbishop of St Andrews, accused of involvement in the murder of Darnley, was hanged there. In the same year Darnley's father, the old Earl of Lennox, regent for his infant grandson during Mary's captivity, was shot in a skirmish at Stirling; and his successor, Regent Mar, died there in the following year.

Prince Henry, the beloved eldest son of James vi who had been baptized with such pomp and ceremony in the chapel royal, died at nineteen, leaving the succession open to the second son, Charles i. With the union of the crowns of England and Scotland in 1603 the king and court removed to London, and in spite of the promise of regular homecomings, the upkeep of the castle began to be neglected. James vi was the last king to live in residence.

The castle was captured and held by the Covenanters in 1651 and yet again was besieged by the English. In 1745 Bonnie Prince Charlie in his retreat northwards made preparations to retrieve the castle, but the battle of Falkirk meant the siege was prolonged until the advance of the Duke of Cumberland's army compelled retreat and led to the tragedy of Culloden. Since that time the castle has remained unassailed.

# 4

## THE PLACE OF SAFETY: DUMBARTON

*Dumbarton Castle in the west of Scotland was both a well nigh impregnable fortress and a convenient gateway to France.*

*I*n February 1548 the five-year-old queen arrived at Dumbarton Castle. She was not to leave it for five months, and when she did so it was to say goodbye to Scotland for thirteen years. Awaiting her in France would be her own kin on her mother's side, the powerful Guise family, and the family of her future husband, the royal house of Valois.

Dumbarton Castle, on its rock in the Firth of Clyde, was the most important strategic castle in the west of Scotland, with a long and turbulent history to match its position. Factual information about its origins dissolves hazily into unproven and unprovable legend. It may have been occupied by the Romans as far back as the first century, during the Antonine period: the wall built by them during the reign of that emperor, stretching across central Scotland in an unsuccessful attempt to extend the frontiers of the Roman Empire, ends in the vicinity of Dumbarton, and it is difficult not to conjecture that the Romans saw the potential of the rock. Like so many other parts of Britain of obvious antiquarian interest, it also claims Arthurian connections, and in addition it holds a place in legend as the birthplace of St Patrick, the patron saint of Ireland. Many other traditions surround the history of Dumbarton but, attractive as they are, no firm evidence supports them, and some indeed have been shown to be the brainchild of dubious sources in very much later centuries.

Dumbarton was originally the capital of the ancient kingdom of Strathclyde. Indeed, the original name for the latter was 'Alclut', which in the language shared by the Britons of that kingdom and by the Welsh, means 'Rock of the Clyde'. In other words, the whole realm seems to have been named after its most strategic settlement. Strathclyde ultimately stretched far beyond the bounds of the region which today bears its name – from Loch Lomondside to Morecambe Bay. It was eventually absorbed into the united Scottish kingdom in 1034.

Dumbarton itself appears in the scanty chronicles of Scottish history in a charter of 1222, when Alexander II records the building of 'my' new castle, and the founding of a royal burgh. Thus Dumbarton firmly entered the royal holdings in Scotland: a most important acquisition providing a western outpost of authority. The king's lieutenant there was the sheriff of Dumbarton, who combined his duties in the burgh with the post of keeper of the castle.

Of the early incumbents one of the most noteworthy was Sir John Menteith, whose name is or was familiar to all Scots schoolchildren as the notorious betrayer, in 1305, of the patriot William Wallace. How Wallace was captured is not clear, but Menteith's complicity and indeed initiative in the episode is without doubt, for he subsequently received £100 from Edward I and, temporarily, the earldom of Lennox. Wallace is reputed to have spent a few days in custody within the walls of Dumbarton Castle on his way to a rigged trial and shameful execution in London; given the fact that his captor was keeper of Dumbarton, this seems likely to be true.

But 'a martyr's life begins with his death', and the trial and death of William Wallace inspired Robert the Bruce to carry on his work for the liberation of Scotland. Once Menteith was himself liberated from his vow of allegiance to Edward by the latter's death, he transferred his loyalty to Bruce and acknowledged his kingship. He did not waver again. But Bruce had staunch allies of longer standing, and it was one of these, Malcolm, Earl Lennox, whom he rewarded with the hereditary offices of sheriff of Dumbarton and keeper of its castle. It was from the Earl of Lennox, too, that Bruce acquired the lands nearby where he spent the last two years of his life, sick with leprosy, frustrated in his desire to lead a crusade to the Holy Land, but surely content in the achievement of his life's work, with the guarantee of Scottish independence under the terms of the hard-won Treaty of Northampton.

Dumbarton continued to have a colourful history suited to its importance. It was one of the very few castles spared from Bruce's policy of dismantling such fortresses: its inaccessibility from England made it unlikely that an invading force would use it as a base for control of the surrounding countryside. By the fifteenth century, Dumbarton had also developed as an important gateway to traffic with France.

In March 1436 a strangely prophetic scene was played out at Dumbarton. The little daughter of James I and his queen, Joan Beaufort, like so many children of royalty and the nobility, was destined to be a pawn on the chessboard of European politics. In 1428, at the age of three, she had been pledged in marriage to the five-year-old Dauphin of France. Eight years and much politicking passed: it is tempting to think, comfortingly, that James and Joan were reluctant to let their daughter go. But an English attempt to forestall the marriage altogether forced their hand, and at Dumbarton they parted with Princess Margaret, then aged eleven, amid scenes of great public splendour and equally great personal distress. James and Joan's marriage had been a love-match, after a highly romantic courtship during James's imprisonment in England. It had inspired from him some fine poetry, and it is particularly moving to imagine them sending their daughter in tears to a country and a husband she had never seen. Unlike Mary Stuart, Princess Margaret found happiness neither with her new country nor with her teenage husband. Her delicate health was undermined by homesickness, and she died nine years later.

Acting keepers and sheriffs continued to be appointed by the crown, but the hereditary title now rested firmly with the earls of Lennox. During Mary's minority it passed into the unreliable hands of the young man who in later years was to be her father-in-law: Matthew, Earl Lennox. His behaviour during this period boded ill for the future.

Matthew appeared in Scotland early in 1543, after eleven years spent in the French king's Scots guard: he was twenty-seven. Mary of Guise and her adviser Cardinal Beaton assumed him to be a francophile and therefore sympathetic to their own views; and they certainly saw in him a potential check to the ambitions of the Earl of Arran, regent for the infant queen. The two earls shared a claim to the Scottish throne through their mutual ancestor Mary, daughter of James II and the brave and lusty Mary of Guelders. Lennox traced his lineage through a grandmother, Arran through his father, so, on the face of it, it would seem that the latter had an undisputed claim on the title already awarded him by Parliament – that of 'second person', or next in line to the throne. But there was a dubious divorce in Arran's background, which put in question the legitimacy of his succession and at the same time elevated Lennox's ambitions.

It must have been with high hopes, therefore, that the queen and the cardinal anticipated the arrival of Lennox at Dumbarton, where with all due solemnity he was handed the keys by the acting keeper. His initial moves showed him, as expected, to be firmly in the French party, and Arran was inundated with demands from Henry VIII to check his rival's power and activities, and especially to achieve the surrender of the key stronghold of Dumbarton. That Lennox was deemed worthy of the utmost confidence by the queen and Beaton, on the other hand, is shown by an incident in October 1543, when a consignment of badly needed French gold crowns arrived at Dumbarton. Out of 10,000, 4,000 of them went to Mary of Guise, 2,000 were divided between the deserving and impoverished loyal Border lords, 2,000 found their way to the cardinal – and the remaining 2,000 were entrusted to Lennox.

*Margaret Douglas, Countess of Lennox. The daughter of Queen Margaret Tudor by her second husband, she was an ambitious woman who pressed the suit of her son Henry from an early age.*

But Lennox was playing a subtle and deceitful game. He had become aware that, as so often in those times, his career prospects would be advanced by a judicious marriage. His quarry was Lady Margaret Douglas, daughter of James IV's queen by her second marriage to the Earl of Angus, and thus the niece of Henry VIII. Lady Margaret had been in attendance at her uncle's court since the age of fifteen, no doubt with a view to fostering her claim to the English succession. At the time such a claim must have seemed more tenuous than subsequent events proved it to be. After all, though nearing the end of his over-indulged life, Henry had three children by his many marriages: it could not have been anticipated that there would be no grandchildren to carry on his line. Still, the uniting of two apparently tenuous links with two different crowns must have had its own attractions for the ambitious man, no matter what the lady's personal qualities might turn out to be.

At the same time Lennox was involved in a bizarre courtship of Mary of Guise, in which he was encouraged by Beaton and the French ambassadors and rivalled by Patrick Hepburn, third Earl of Bothwell. A contemporary account of their attempts to woo the twenty-five-year-old widow has the ring of a twentieth-century gossip columnist: 'they daily pursued the court and the queen mother with bravery, singing, dancing and playing on instruments, arrayed every day in sundry habilliments and prided who should be the most gallant in their clothing'. The intelligent and strong-willed woman must have laughed at their posturings. Bothwell was not even free to pursue such a courtship: did she encourage him? If so, did she feel responsible when in the autumn of 1543 he cast aside his wife on the ever-convenient grounds of consanguinity, the better to pursue her?

What she could not have foreseen was that by a cruel irony of fortune the sons of these two men would one after the other marry her daughter, between them guiding her along the path to breakdown, scandal, abdication, captivity and execution. For Mary's sake, though probably not for her own personal happiness, she might with hindsight have been wise to

accept the devious advances of Matthew Lennox. But she refused them, or adroitly avoided them, and he turned with greater assiduity to the option of Lady Margaret Douglas. He married her in 1544, pledging himself to be Henry's man and to surrender Dumbarton Castle; and he spawned Henry, Lord Darnley.

But Lennox had reckoned without the man who had handed him the keys on his arrival at the castle the previous year: George Stirling of Glorat. Untempted by the offer of an English bribe, he refused to break the trust that James v had placed in him, and thus thwarted Lennox's projected role in Henry's 'rough wooing'. While Hertford's savage despoliation of the eastern Border continued, Henry's new nephew by marriage was to have established an English outpost on the west. Stirling of Glorat held it successfully, however, and though Dumbarton continued to be a focus of military activity, by July 1546 it was firmly in the hands of the Earl of Arran.

By the summer of 1547 the English had advanced northwards with renewed savagery, undeflected by the death of Henry VIII. An army under the new protector of the English realm, Somerset, inflicted a humiliating and crushing defeat at Pinkie Cleugh, near Musselburgh, on a Scots force that was superior in numbers and inferior in morale and leadership. English garrisons were established as far north as Tayside, and Haddington – only eighteen miles from Edinburgh – was also in their hands. But on the west, Lennox had again failed to effect a corresponding invasion, and it was at this stage, in February 1548, that Mary of Guise deemed it wise to remove her daughter to the apparent impregnability of Dumbarton Castle.

She was closely guarded there, by French soldiers rather than Scots, but the immediate danger was less from foreign attack than from childhood illness. There is conflicting evidence as to whether this was measles or a mild smallpox virus, but at any rate she was sufficiently ill for rumours of her death to sweep the countryside. If the disease was smallpox it certainly was of a strain weak enough to leave her skin unmarked, but it would account for her apparent lack of fear later, when she nursed Darnley through similar diseases.

At last the longed-for French help arrived, but it was conditional. In July 1548, at a nunnery near Haddington, a treaty was signed between the Scots and the French agreeing *inter alia* to the marriage of Mary to the young Dauphin of France; in return Scotland came under the protection, if not the suzerainty, of the King of France:

... the which day Monsieur d'Esse, Lieutenant general of the navy and army sent by the most Christian king of France for support of this Realm at this present time, show ... that the said most Christian king had set his whole heart and mind for defence of this Realm, desired in his said master's name for the more perfect union and indissoluble bond of perpetual amity and confederation the marriage of our Sovereign Lady to the effect that the said most Christian king's eldest son and Dauphin of France may be joined in marriage with her Grace ... observing and keeping this realm and the lieges thereof as has been in all kings of Scotland in all time past; and shall maintain and defend this Realm and the lieges thereof the same as he does the Realm of France and lieges thereof ...

Little time elapsed between the signing of the treaty and the departure of the young queen and her train from Dumbarton. They had boarded the French royal galley by the end of the month. Mary was leaving her mother, who must have been a shadowy figure to her, but she was in the company of those much more familiar figures of her childhood, her guardians. With her, too, was her governess and aunt, Lady Fleming (who became so ill in the gales that bound the fleet to the Firth of Clyde for a week that she begged to return to land for a rest, only to be told by the outspoken captain that she would go to France and like it, or drown on the voyage, but under no circumstances would she be put ashore). It was at this point, too, that those supporting characters of every novel about Mary Queen of Scots make

*The battlefield of Pinkie Cleugh, near Musselburgh. After the defeat of the Scots army there, the question of Mary's removal to France was more vigorously pursued.*

their first public appearance: the four Maries. Myth sees them as torn from the bosom of their families to begin a lifetime of service to their mistress; but Mary Fleming was accompanied by her widowed mother, and Mary Livingstone and Mary Beaton were with their fathers and presumably also their French mothers.

Behind Mary Stuart lay an insecure crown and a rebellious kingdom. Ahead lay the splendours of the French court. France was half her heritage, and her adoption of it was wholehearted. She was to spend longer there than in her own land, both as a child and as a woman, and after she left its shores she would never really find happiness again.

Arran (now, under the Treaty of Haddington, Duke of Châtelherault), continued to hold Dumbarton and, now that the queen's future appeared to be in France, guarded his position as 'second person' all the more jealously. For years Mary of Guise had dangled the prospect of a match between her daughter and Châtelherault's son – now known as 'young Arran' – before the Hamiltons. Twelve years later the early death of Francis II gave young Arran's fantasies, fuelled by family and personal ambition alike, a new lease of life, and he started to pay suit to Mary while she was still in mourning for her husband.

But such indelicacy was as nothing compared with his scheme to abduct her to Dumbarton Castle in 1562. It is difficult to distinguish truth from fantasy in this episode. Arran implicated both his father and Bothwell, with whom he was habitually on unfriendly terms: a recent rapprochement may only have been part of a more sinister long-term plan. But whose? By that time Arran had undoubtedly tipped over the precipice beyond reason, but nevertheless had a lunatic's cunning. The case against Bothwell depends not on any reliable contemporary evidence but on the fact that five years later he did indeed abduct the queen. At best it remains not proven. Any judgement on the balance of probabilities can only rest on an overall assessment of each earl's character and motives.

But at any rate, the madman's ravings suited the policy of Mary's half-brother, Lord James Stewart, only too well: Arran, for his own safety as well as that of others, was carefully warded till his death in 1609, long after that of any of the other participants in the episode; Bothwell was meanwhile imprisoned without charge or trial; and Châtelherault was forced to surrender the guardianship of Dumbarton Castle.

In 1565 it seemed likely that with Mary's marriage to her cousin Darnley, Dumbarton would be restored to the Lennox faction, and in particular to her father-in-law, Matthew. But however besotted she was with the son, she must have had a residual and quite justified distrust of the father, for she placed the castle in the reliable and faithful hands of another cousin, Lord Fleming – another descendant of the extramarital union between James IV and the Countess of Bothwell. Three years later, after Darnley's death and her subsequent marriage to Bothwell, it was to Dumbarton that Mary made her way after her escape from Lochleven, only to have her route cut off by Moray's troops after his victory at Langside.

Fleming continued to hold Dumbarton on Mary's behalf until 1571, although under heavy pressure from Lennox, and the castle became the focus of resistance for the party of Marian supporters. In the spring of that year, however, after a six-month truce, it was captured in a daring raid led by Captain Thomas Crawford of Jordanhill. With its fall went the last real hope of Mary's restoration.

Dumbarton Castle continued to play a significant role in the affairs of Scotland for the remainder of the sixteenth century and during the Wars of the Covenant of the next one. And unlike the other places which played their parts in Mary's reign, Dumbarton again bore the brunt of enemy attack this century. It was the naval ships at Denny's Yards and the nearby aircraft factory that were the targets of two successive nights of heavy German bombing in May 1941, but the buildings on the rock, too, added to their battle scars when they were hit by four high-explosive bombs.

OPPOSITE *'The Queen of Scots is the most perfect child,' enthused Mary's future father-in-law on her arrival in France. This anonymous portrait shows the child who capitivated the French court.*

BELOW *Francis II, Mary's first husband and the playmate of her childhood years, by François Clouet. If their love was immature, it was also genuine and forged out of personal need as much as political dictates.*

# 5

# *EDINBURGH:*
# *PORT AND CASTLE*

*Edinburgh Castle,
dominating the old city today
as it did in the sixteenth
century. Here Mary's son,
the future James VI and I,
was born in 1566.*

It was thirteen years later, in August 1561, that Mary returned to her own country. Her glorious girlhood, happy marriage and brief queenship in France were now behind her. She had been petted by her father-in-law and her uncles, on whom she had been able to rely completely for political guidance. Basking in the adoration of her frail adolescent husband, she had been garlanded with tributes by courtiers and artists. Now she was returning to her unknown inheritance, whose future she had hitherto only considered in relation to her adopted country. The secret treaty of April 1558, by which she had virtually given Scotland to France on her marriage to the dauphin, illustrates at best the power of her Guise uncles and, at worst her lack of interest in her native land. The death of Francis before her and also before the birth of any heirs had forestalled the implementation of the treaty's conditions; but the triumvirate of the Duke of Châtelherault, the Earl of Arran and Lord James Stewart, whose rule she was now interrupting in Scotland, was aware of its existence.

On the throne of England was her cousin Elizabeth, a cool and competent young woman who had survived a hazardous youth to succeed at last to her father's crown. Elizabeth had supported the Protestant Scots lords in their successful revolt against Mary of Guise in 1560, and was unlikely to be generously disposed towards her daughter. Added to the religious difference between the two queens was Mary's insulting claim, instigated by her Guise uncles, to the 'triple crown' – Scotland, France and England. This claim threw Elizabeth's legitimacy into dispute: small wonder then that Mary's return was frustrated by difficulties over such matters as the issue of an English passport.

Ironically, her sad return on a foggy August day was to the very port where, the previous year, the troops of her dying mother, defeated by Protestant Scots and English forces, had finally lost the struggle against the Reformation in Scotland. Leith stands at the mouth of the water that bears its name, a couple of miles to the south-east of Edinburgh. There had been religious foundations and a port there from early times, but it was after the devastation of Berwick in the fourteenth century, and its later annexation by England, that Leith rose in importance to become Scotland's principal trading port. Throughout the Middle Ages a busy trade was carried on with Norway and the Low Countries and, as the French alliance strengthened, with France as well. But, though a burgh in its own right, Leith could not take the profit from such trade, for this right was reserved for royal burghs. And Edinburgh guarded its privileges jealously, causing feeling between the two burghs to run high.

In the early sixteenth century James IV was engaged in building up a Scottish navy. Leith was conveniently placed for the work but the river mouth there was too shallow, so a shipyard was established just along the river at Newhaven, where some of the great ships of the Scottish navy were constructed, among them the *Great Michael*. Many were manned by Leith sailors, renowned for their ferocity which, though it sometimes earned them condemnation as pirates, was also an asset. When at about this time five English ships

*A portrait by Clouet of Mary in mourning clothes, probably for her father-in-law Henri II. The subsequent death of her husband forced her reluctant return to Scotland in 1561*

entered the Firth of Forth and caused great destruction along the shores of Fife and the Lothians, James IV ordered Sir Andrew Wood to pursue them in his ships, the *Yellow Carvel* and the *Flower*. Under his expert captaincy the Scots caught the rogue ships off the coast of Dunbar where, in spite of the unequal odds and after hours of battling over hulls locked together with grappling irons, the skill of the Leith sailors prevailed. The five captured ships were brought back in triumph.

Another noted seagoing Leith family was the Bartons of Barnton. Sir Andrew Barton often harassed English ships 'by mistake', under the pretext of recovering pirated goods from Portuguese vessels. Eventually he provoked them to retaliation, and after a prolonged sea battle he was killed and his beloved ship the *Lion* removed to London. There it was renamed the *Great Harry* and became the largest man-of-war in the English navy.

*The port of Leith, by which Mary returned to Scotland, was Scotland's major trading port. Its siege in 1560 marked the triumph of the forces of Protestantism.*

Two queens consort among Queen Mary's ancestors had taken their first steps on Scottish soil at Leith. Over a century earlier Mary of Guelders, newly arrived from the Low Countries to marry James II, had been met by a vast array of nobility, and taken through the streets to her royal reception in Edinburgh riding pillion (sidesaddles were not introduced into Scotland until Mary Stuart's reign). Twenty years later, in 1468, her daughter-in-law, Princess Margaret of Denmark, arrived at the self-same place to marry James III, bringing with her a dowry from her impecunious father not of money, but of the Orkney and Shetland Isles. Her escort for the occasion was the Earl of Arran, who in his absence had incurred the king's wrath, and who was therefore returning, unsuspecting, to imprisonment. Desperate to save him, the Countess of Arran – who was the king's sister – managed to board the princess's vessel and warn her husband, and together they escaped to Denmark.

LEFT *Carved wooden panels believed to have been in the chapel used by Mary of Guise at Leith. They are now in the chapel at Traquair House, near Peebles.*

BELOW *Also at Traquair is the cradle of the infant James VI.*

Both these foreign princesses had stepped ashore at the King's Wark, a great building standing at the mouth of the harbour. Built by James I as a storage place for goods destined for the court, it later developed into the country's principal arsenal. Like the rest of Leith, it suffered badly in Henry VIII's 'rough wooing' of 1544.

On Sunday 4 May of that year, 10,000 men under the ruthless command of the Earl of Hertford docked at Granton, with these chilling orders: 'Sack Leith, and burn and subvert it, and all the rest, putting man, woman, and child to fire and sword without exception, when any resistance shall be made against you.' Resistance was not offered, Leith being totally unprepared for the invasion. Having arrived at midday, the English replenished themselves from the larders of the burgh before continuing into Edinburgh, leaving a force of over a thousand to hold Leith until their return. Although they failed to take Edinburgh Castle they carried out Henry's vindictive policy to the full, leaving the city in ruins. Back in Leith they sacked and looted all they could, destroying the rest by fire, including the wooden pier.

Three years later, and only months after the death of Henry, Hertford, now Protector Somerset, was preparing a repeat performance. This time the Scottish Privy Council, meeting in Edinburgh, were determined to be ready. Emergency signals in the form of the 'fiery cross' were sent out to every village, and this time help hastened to Edinburgh from all over Scotland. Thirty-six thousand men and members of the Catholic clergy gathered there to prepare for battle. On 10 September 1547 the English army reached Pinkie Cleugh and the two sides engaged, but under weak command, and forgetting their carefully laid plans the Scottish army fell into disarray and suffered a disastrous defeat. Throughout the following week the English rampaged through Edinburgh and the surrounding country-side, implementing their 'scorched earth' policy, and again Leith was burned to the ground.

A dozen years later, under pressure from her French relatives to hold Scotland against the Protestant lords, Mary of Guise attempted to safeguard the position of her French troops in Leith. Hoping to maintain the allegiance of the people of the town she offered to grant them the privilege they had long hoped for – that of becoming a royal burgh, which would enable them to trade abroad. To this end Leith raised £3,600 Scots and made it over to Mary on the understanding that in return she would fulfil her promise without delay. By 1559 nothing had happened, and in the ensuing chaos of the Reformation the granting of Leith's privilege was forgotten.

In need of a safe retreat, Mary gave orders for a great earth wall to be thrown up around Leith and had a house built for herself in what is now Water Street. In October 1559 she took up residence here but, sick at heart as well as in spirit, she stayed only a month before returning to Edinburgh. In the spring of 1560 the English army arrived to support the Protestant cause and, having gathered their forces at Restalrig the day after Palm Sunday, began the siege of Leith. The wall proved a sturdy barrier, strong and high enough to prevent the guns from inflicting any real damage, while the six stone-built ports withstood all attempts to gain entry. The Lords of the Congregation were determined to root out the French, however, and soon responded by building three mounds outside the wall to give their guns a clear firing line. On Easter Sunday the guns opened fire on the buildings below: the tower of the preceptory and the central tower of the church collapsed, amidst the prayers of the people of Leith.

The French remained entrenched, although growing increasingly desperate and with no sign of help. On 11 June, with the death of Mary of Guise, hostilities ceased, and on 6 July 1560 France and England signed the Treaty of Leith. It was agreed that both countries would withdraw and pursue a policy of non-interference, and that Queen Mary and her husband Francis would abstain from using the arms of England. Although religion was not mentioned specifically in the treaty, concessions were to be granted in this direction. With good government established, it was agreed that Queen Mary's French deputies would desist from interfering in matters of religion brought before Parliament. With power thus assured to the Protestants, the way was paved for the Scottish Reformation.

At nine o'clock in the morning of 19 August 1561 Mary Queen of Scots arrived at Leith, somewhat earlier than expected. The circumstances were less than auspicious. The welcoming party was late, and the galley holding the magnificent horses on which she had planned to make her entry into the capital had been impounded by the English. She was welcomed by the provost of Leith and dined at his house. Eventually she and her party, accompanied by Moray and the Scots lords, made their way on inferior borrowed nags towards her new life.

If the approach to Edinburgh has changed, the dominant view of it is still as stunning today as it must have been to Mary. Even in her infancy she had never been further east in Scotland than Linlithgow, but in any case nearly all her memories must have been of France, and the only castles she knew were the pleasure palaces along the Loire. Like those at Stirling and Dumbarton, Edinburgh's castle is a fortress, incomparably sited both for spectacle and security. It was to become a part of the story of her life, as it had been of her ancestors and of her nation far back into history.

The city itself was originally the capital of a Celtic tribe called the Goddoddin. It was known as 'Dinas Eidyn', which was later translated into Gaelic as 'Dun Eadainn' (or Dunedin, as New Zealand today prefers), and then reversed and anglicized to become Edinburgh. The earliest surviving building within the castle walls is the small chapel of St Margaret, built by the pious queen of Malcolm Canmore, first king of a united Scotland. Soldiers stationed in the castle today can still use the eleventh-century chapel for marriage and baptismal services.

Queen Margaret died on hearing the news of the deaths in battle of her husband and son, and what happened thereafter forms the first of the legends of the castle. Her body was prepared for burial at Dunfermline Abbey – one of her many religious foundations – but before it could be taken there the castle was blockaded by King Malcolm's brother, who judged this time of crisis to be an appropriate moment at which to lay claim to the throne. The only exit was down the steep and treacherous west side of the castle rock but, undaunted, her sons prepared to make this descent with her coffin. Miraculously, a fog descended around the cortège, and they made their way down the rock with their precious burden unseen by their blinded foes.

During the Wars of Independence the capture of Edinburgh Castle from the English became of paramount importance to Robert the Bruce. By 1313 this had still not been achieved: Randolph, Earl Moray, who was entrusted to effect the coup, found it an impossible task. From the impenetrable wall above its well-stocked storehouses the English troops taunted the besiegers camped around its base. Then one of Moray's soldiers proposed a highly hazardous plan.

Twenty years earlier, as a young man living in the castle, he had been frustrated in his desire to visit a maiden living in the West Bow by the practice of closing the castle gates at dusk. Recklessly he had devised a way of clambering up and down the cliff face at night by means of a rope ladder and a series of ledges that he had discovered. Now, on a bitterly cold March night, he proposed to lead a small band up his secret route to surprise the sentinels. Stealthily, the thirty armed men began the perilous ascent of the 200-foot cliff face, pulling themselves hand over hand up the icy rock. They reached the base of the castle walls exhausted, but, wasting no time, they bound their ladders together and heaved themselves over, giving the bewildered garrison no time to collect themselves. As was his policy, Bruce

*Another view of Edinburgh Castle. The last attack on it during the many centuries of its history came when it was captured from adherents of Mary's cause in 1573.*

stripped the castle of its defences, leaving only the tiny chapel of St Margaret untouched.

For twenty-five years the castle rock lay desolate, affording no protection to Edward II who was compelled to retreat after sacking the city, or to the army of Edward III, sent to take possession of Edinburghshire six years after the signing of the Treaty of Northampton had been ratified, confirming the independence of Scotland. On this occasion the Earl of Moray again defeated the English, this time on the Borough Moor, before chasing the unfortunate survivors headlong into Edinburgh, where many were slaughtered in the narrow wynds and lanes.

By 1337, however, Edward III had regained control of the south of Scotland, and rebuilt Edinburgh Castle and placed a strong garrison in it. Four years later another daring plot to win the castle back for Scotland was being hatched, this time by Sir William Douglas, the Knight of Liddesdale. The plan depended on the famous greed of the castle governor. An ex-priest disguised as the captain of an English trading vessel sailed into Leith and offered first choice of his French wines and biscuits to the castellan, who bought the whole cargo and ordered it to be delivered early next morning. As the first cart pulled under the portcullis, escorted by twelve hooded seamen, it was overturned, preventing the grating from descending. The seamen were transmogrified into soldiers, and their ranks were swelled by Douglas's waiting men. After the capture of the castle the Scottish banner was raised, never again to be lowered in Edinburgh until the Act of Union of 1707.

It was Bruce's son, David II, who completed the restoration work of the castle. His architect was the future Robert III, who was familiar with the latest French style in fortifications. He was responsible for building 'David's Tower' on the north side of the castle, where King David died in 1370, the last of the short line of Bruce kings. It was this tower above all, nearly sixty feet high and protected by three doors and a pit, which made the castle utterly impregnable to subsequent invasions and sieges.

After the murder of James I at Perth, his son, James II, was brought up mainly at Edinburgh Castle. It was he who really reinstated Edinburgh as the capital of Scotland, a status that was never again challenged. It was from Edinburgh Castle that James II went to his coronation in 1437 at the tender age of seven, to find himself thereafter a pawn and a prisoner in the hands of the competing Scots lords, all of whom wished to rule through possession of him. It was a pattern to be repeated again and again in Scottish history. Fortunately the widow of the first James, like several of her successors, was an intelligent and a resourceful woman.

After two years the Lord Chancellor, Crichton, began to refuse anyone else permission to see James, and Queen Joan made plans to remove the boy. She sought protection in the castle and after some weeks took her leave, tearfully beseeching Crichton to look after her young son. Unknown to him, however, she had packed the boy into a small chest which was then strapped to one of her baggage horses, and in this way smuggled him out of the castle and down to Leith, whence he was shipped to Stirling where Regent Livingstone was waiting. Before long, however, Livingstone began to use the king in the same manner as Crichton, compelling the queen to steal back her son once more and flee to Edinburgh and the eager arms of Crichton. Livingstone followed with his forces and civil war seemed imminent. The two sides were reconciled in the church of St Giles, however, by the bishops who encouraged them both to make war against the Douglases.

It was in November 1440 that the most notorious piece of treachery was perpetrated within the castle walls. The lieutenant governor of Scotland, the great Earl of Douglas, had just died, leaving to his two sons, William and David, wealth and vassals equal to the king's. The elder brother was arrogant for his eighteen years, and his practice of riding out with a following of 1,500 mail-clad warriors led to his being cited as an enemy to the throne. The two brothers were invited to a council in Edinburgh, and were warmly welcomed at the castle, although their entourage was excluded for lack of room. The child king was charmed with his young guests and a feast was set forth. All went well until the main meal was served, when, under the shocked gaze of the king and the two young brothers, the head of a black bull was carried to the table. Under ancient Scottish custom, this presaged the death of the principal guest. The young men put up a fight, and the king begged for their lives to be spared; but after a mock trial they were beheaded. The treachery was commemorated in a popular rhyme:

> Edinburgh Castle, town and tower,
> God grant thou sink for sin
> And that even for the black dinner
> Earl Douglas gat therein.

The great banqueting hall where this outrage was perpetrated is still used for state receptions and banquets.

In spite of the horrors of his childhood, James II continued to live mainly at Edinburgh Castle after his marriage to Mary of Guelders. It was he who created the Nor' Loch, an artificial loch, first defensive and then purely decorative, which was a notable feature of Edinburgh until it was drained at the end of the eighteenth century when the New Town was built. In its place now lie Princes Street Gardens and the rail network that runs into Waverley Station. It was at this time, too, that the famous cannon known as Mons Meg made its appearance, the largest, most powerful cannon ever seen. It is generally believed to have been forged in Flanders – hence its name – but some claim that it was built in Galloway, the work of a blacksmith and his seven sons. It was not used solely for war or like purposes: on 24 April 1558 the great gun boomed out in celebration of the marriage of Mary Stuart to the dauphin. James II's interest in armaments was to be the cause of his early death, however, for he was killed at the siege of Roxburgh Castle by the explosion of one of his own cannon.

Before he began the construction of Holyrood Palace in about 1500, James IV presided over glittering occasions at the castle. There was jousting in the castle lists at the south-western corner of its base, and the court watched the proceedings from the battlements. One of the most celebrated of these encounters took place in 1503, when a knight from the Low Countries challenged 'the best knight in Scotland' to fight with him to the death. The challenge was taken up by Sir Patrick Hamilton; fighting with two-handed swords followed combat on horseback, and only the king's intervention prevented the death of the challenger. Inside the castle, the hand of the great king can still be seen in the hammer-beam roof of the great banqueting hall, constructed in the form of an inverted ship's hull and decorated with human and animal masks like those at Stirling.

Like his great-grandfather, during his minority James V was tossed to and fro among the nobles like a shuttlecock in the game of power, but without his ancestor's advantage of a wise mother. From this time Edinburgh Castle was used increasingly as a prison for political prisoners: nearly all the Border lairds seem to have spent some time within its walls. In his later years James V added to the defences of the castle with walls, towers and an increase in cannon power.

During the period of the 'rough wooing' the castle successfully resisted the attacks of the English forces under the Earl of Hertford in 1544 and 1547. Shortly after the English had once more withdrawn, leaving the town in ruins, Mary of Guise began to build herself a new residence on the castle hill. It stood where the Church of Scotland Assembly Hall now stands, close enough to the castle to be protected by its guns. Although it was not so grand as Holyrood, the widowed queen must have felt safer here, now that the waves of the Reformation were beginning to rock the troubled burgh.

In 1560, ill and worn out by the troubles, homesick for her native land and with her troops in Leith about to be overcome, she turned in desperation to the leaders of the opposing party in the castle and begged shelter there for herself and her ladies. On 1 April this was granted. Though only forty-four, she was now suffering from an advanced form of dropsy and, bent double, was able to hobble about the courtyard only with the aid of a staff. Her agony was heightened six days later, on the eve of Palm Sunday, when from the castle walls she watched her own forces being driven back by the allied Scottish and English troops in the battle which took place between Restalrig and Leith. Two weeks later the dying queen regent was unable to rise from her bed and, wishing to make amends, she summoned all the nobles to make a last appeal to them for unity, and the good of the country.

Not all of them turned up. Some, influenced by John Knox, felt it unwise in case the 'Guisian practice should prevail' and the dying queen should 'enchant' them. After begging their forgiveness for her part in the wars and embracing them, she fell into a coma and died early in the morning of 11 June, twenty-two years to the day after her arrival in Scotland. She had struggled for most of that time with the problems of her adopted country, and since the death of Cardinal Beaton had pursued her remedies to them almost single-handed.

*Mary of Guise died at Edinburgh Castle in 1560, having lived to see the defeat of her pro-French, pro-Catholic policy for Scotland. This portrait is attributed to Corneille de Lyon.*

With the hindsight of centuries, it is clear that she was making a stand against forces of change as relentless as the revolution that was to sweep her native France over two centuries later. It is possible to criticize her policies, for if she had been less pro-French and pro-Catholic, if she had accepted as inevitable the march of the Reformation, and understood that a French subordination was as unacceptable to the Scots lords as an English one – if she had been capable of all this, she might have left a secure throne to her daughter. But perhaps this would have required superhuman wisdom and foresight, for to contemporary eyes the future of the nation did not even include the return of its regnant queen.

She did her best, however, and she was a strong woman, who in astuteness, ability and self-reliance stood head and shoulders above her daughter. Set in the outside wall of the royal apartments at Edinburgh Castle, between the crown room and the banqueting hall, is a stone tablet bearing her epitaph:

Mary of Lorraine, Queen of James v, Mother of Mary Queen of Scots, and Regent of Scotland from 1554–1560, died here 11 June 1560. A lady of honourable condition – of singular judgement – full of humanity – a great lover of justice – helpful to the poor.

It was three days after Mary Stuart's arrival in Leith over a year later that she entered the castle and dined there. Her progress from Holyrood had been triumphant, and she was met at the gates of the city's leading burgesses. After dinner, she left the castle to be treated to some highly propagandist street theatre, as described to William Cecil by Randolph, the English ambassador:

A boy of six . . . presented unto her a Bible and a Psalter, and spake unto her the verses which I send you. Then, for the terrible significations of God upon idolatory, there were burnt Korah, Dathan, and Abiram, in the time of their sacrifice. They were minded to have a priest burned at the altar, at the elevation.

As in the days of her father, in the early years of Mary's reign Edinburgh Castle was used primarily as a prison. The most notable of its prisoners was the Earl of Bothwell, who was incarcerated there in 1562. As we have seen, Bothwell had been implicated by the Earl of Arran in a plot to kidnap the queen in order to force a marriage with the latter. The episode marked the point at which Arran's instability tipped over into insanity. The truth of the incident, clouded by accusations, withdrawals and Bothwell's expressions of complete innocence, has never been determined. But on the strength of a madman's word Bothwell, whose record of loyalty to both Mary and her mother was impeccable, was imprisoned without trial. After four months in Edinburgh Castle, enlisting the help of the Captain's servant, he pulled out a bar from his window and made his escape down the castle rock.

After the horrific murder of her favourite servant, Rizzio, at Holyrood in March 1566, Mary could not face giving birth to her child in a place which harboured such memories and, given the instability of the country, the castle was a much safer place at a time when she and her baby would be so vulnerable. It was turned back into a royal palace, and furnished accordingly. The polished oak floors were covered with sixteen Turkish carpets, and elaborately carved massive oak tables were installed, with chairs covered with gilded leather and cushions of brocade and damask. It is said that Mary had 'eleven tapestries of gilded leather, eight of the Judgement of Paris, five of the Triumph of Virtue; eight of green velvet, ten of cloth of gold and brocaded taffeta; thirty more of massive cloth of gold, one bearing the story of the Comte de Foix, eight bearing the ducal arms of Longueville, five having the history of King Rehoboam, one the tale of Tobit, and four the Hunts of the Unicorn'.

Mary's tiny bedchamber, only eight feet at its longest, is the most moving and intimate room in the castle. It was here that Mary's mother died, and her son James vi was born. Though her bed was hung with golden cloth, this little room, panelled in wainscot, with a dark-painted ceiling and small barred window, seems a sombre choice for a queen. On the roof panels are painted the initials of mother and son, M.R. and I.R., and on the wall the date of the child's birth, the royal Stuart coat of arms, and below, a prayer:

Lord Jesu Chryst that crounit was with thornse
Preserve the birth quhais bedgie heir is borne
And send hir sonne successione to reign still
Lang in this realme, if that be thy will
Als grant, O Lord quhatever of hir proseed
Be to thy glorie honer and prais sobeid.

James vi was born on the morning of 19 June 1566. Whatever Mary's feelings were by this stage (for her marriage to Darnley had proved a disastrous mistake), there was much

public rejoicing. The bitter party strife which still split the country was temporarily laid aside. Cannon – Mons Meg the loudest of them all – thundered from the castle walls to announce the glad tidings to the citizens of Edinburgh, while inside the crowded bedchamber Mary was surrounded by the principal noblemen of the realm as she presented the young father with his son. Lord Herries' memoirs describe the scene:

About two o'clock in the afternoon the king came to visit the queen, and was desirous to see the child. 'My Lord,' says the queen, 'God has given you and me a son, begotten by none but you!' At which words the king blushed, and kissed the child. Then she took the child in her arms, and discovering his face, said, 'My Lord, here I protest to God, and as I shall answer to him at the great day of judgement, this is your son, and no other man's son! And I am desirous that all here, with ladies and others, bear witness; for he is so much your son that I fear it will be the worse for him hereafter!' Then she spoke to Sir William Stanley. 'This', says she, 'is the son whom (I hope) shall first unite the two kingdoms of Scotland and England!' Sir William answered, 'Why, Madam? Shall he succeed before your Majesty and his father?' 'Because', says she, 'his father has broken to me.'

At eleven o'clock, only an hour after the birth, Sir James Melville was commissioned to bear the tidings to the English queen in London, riding with such speed that, as he wrote afterwards, 'As it struck twelve I took my horse, and was at Berwick the same night.' Four days later he was in London. The news was not received well: in the same letter Melville recounts how, although Elizabeth was dancing when he arrived, upon his announcement of the birth all merriment ceased, and the queen, sitting down 'with her hand upon her haffit',

ABOVE *The Earl of Morton, who played a significant role in the events of Mary's reign and afterwards became regent to James VI.*

ABOVE LEFT *James VI, the child born at Edinburgh Castle who was to unite the crowns of Scotland and England. A portrait by Arnold Bronckorst.*

exclaimed bitterly to her ladies, 'how the Queen of Scotland was the mother of a fair son, and she but a barren stock'. In Edinburgh, however, joy prevailed. On the night of the prince's birthday bonfires blazed on Calton Hill and Arthur's Seat, and the next day the church of St Giles overflowed with people attending a thanksgiving service.

Early in 1567, Mary removed the command of Edinburgh Castle from its traditional keeper, the Earl of Mar, and entrusted it into the hands of Bothwell's colleague Sir James Balfour. But her trust proved to be misplaced for, in her moment of crisis with the lords after her marriage to Bothwell, James Balfour threw in his lot with the rebels. And shortly after her imprisonment in Lochleven he surrendered to them a piece of ammunition more valuable than any guns. It was a silver casket belonging to Bothwell, and in it were love letters and poems addressed to him by an infatuated mistress.

From that day to this, controversy has raged over whether the letters that were later published and produced at Mary's trial, and which provided the excuse for her years of incarceration in English prisons, were hers, or were written by another mistress, or were careful forgeries. If they were authentic, her complicity in the murder of Darnley is undeniable, as is an adulterous affair of some duration with Bothwell. If they were forgeries, as she claimed, then she is indeed one of the most pathetic victims of a miscarriage of justice.

If at the time of her surrender to the rebel lords at Carberry Hill and of her imprisonment at Lochleven she was failed by the man in charge of Edinburgh Castle, the same cannot be said after her final defeat at Langside and her flight into England. The Scottish nobility was then divided between those who were 'Queen's Men' and those who supported the cause of her son, the 'King's Men'. In the two years that followed the strongholds held by the Queen's Men gradually fell, until finally only Edinburgh Castle remained in their possession. It was held by Sir William Kirkcaldy of Grange, whose disgust at the treatment of the queen had converted him, belatedly, to her cause.

Early in 1570 the attacks on the castle began. For two and a half years the King's Men battered at the massive walls to no avail, Kirkcaldy's forces remaining entrenched inside. All this time a few loyal supporters in the town secretly supplied the garrison with grain by all manner of routes, including an old tunnel running from the castle down under the High Street. The Earl of Mar, who succeeded to Lennox's command of the King's Men, then attempted to starve out Edinburgh by destroying all the mills in the neighbourhood and closing the coal-pits. In answer Kirkcaldy sallied forth into the town, tore down the rafters of his opponents' houses and sold them for firewood.

When Morton succeeded to the regency on the death of Mar the hostilities intensified and as the spring of 1573 wore on the downfall of the castle seemed inevitable. Morton had applied to Queen Elizabeth for help, and fifteen hundred men equipped with massive cannon soon arrived. The enormous guns were erected on batteries, and on 17 May they all opened fire at once, continuing non-stop for nearly a week, when the approach of the end was signalled by the sudden collapse of David's Tower, which had stood solidly for three hundred years. With its destruction, the other towers soon crumbled and the castle was left almost defenceless. Receiving a solemn promise of fair treatment Kirkcaldy marched out of the castle the next day and delivered up his sword to the English commander. Within three months he was publicly hanged at the Mercat Cross in the High Street.

The castle was so ruinous that James VI never lived there, preferring Holyrood. It was refortified, however, by Regent Morton, who built what is now known as the Half Moon Battery over the remains of David's Tower. Much of the castle was again destroyed or removed by Cromwell in 1650. Since the union of the crowns of Scotland and England in 1707 it has been kept in a state of good repair, the only cannon fire to be heard being that of the one o'clock gun.

# 6

# EDINBURGH:
# TOWN AND PALACE

In the sixteenth century Edinburgh was the chief city of Scotland in all respects. It was not only the largest, with thirty thousand inhabitants, but also the wealthiest; the permanent presence of the supreme court of law, the Session, and the regular meetings of Parliament made it the legal and political centre; and the residence of John Knox, that leading voice of the Reformation, assured its predominance in questions of religion. The arrival of Mary Queen of Scots and the establishment of her court at Holyrood made its ascendancy complete.

The main thoroughfare of the old town of Edinburgh straggles down a ridge of land from the castle rock to the foot of the valley a mile to the east. Here lies the second royal residence, Holyrood Palace, and hence this timeless High Street is known as the Royal Mile. This was universally admired in Mary's day, as it bore no resemblance to the dingy, muddy, narrow streets of most medieval towns. It was unique not only for its length and breadth, but also for its great square paving stones.

But if the buildings of the centre, and particularly of this street, gave the town a spacious and stately appearance, the fringes belied this. Clinging to the fronts of the houses were haphazard wooden balconies which projected into the street, with all manner of booths lurking perilously beneath their supporting beams. Rickety forestairs gave access to the dwellings on the first floor, where rough-hewn boards formed the walls with round holes cut for windows, just big enough to allow a person's head through to survey the day's events. Although by 1560 it had been decreed that no house was to be roofed with thatch, to lessen the danger of fire, the indiscriminate piling of tar-barrels, straw, broom and wood in the narrow closes was a constant headache for the authorities. Pigs and other stock were often allowed to forage at will, and if the vennels and side streets were hazardous to traverse at the best of times, the many middens only increased the difficulties. This state of affairs led one visitor to the city to remark that it was like 'an ivory comb whose teeth on both sides are very foul, though the space between them is clean and sightly'.

The numerous closes running off the Royal Mile and the overcrowded streets of the town were the result of the delineation of the town's boundaries by the King's Wall, built in 1450. Under the combined pressures of war and population increase the narrow strips of garden between the houses were built over and extra storeys added on above. But while the people chose to live within the safety of the wall, concessions were given to religious organizations and trades to found their houses in the open land to the south: Greyfriars' Church, St Mary in the Fields (later known as Kirk o'Field), the Convent of St Mary of Placentia (which gave its name to the area now known as the Pleasance), the Candlemaker and Potter Rows all lie in this direction.

In time these extra buildings extended the bounds of the city far beyond the King's Wall, and after 1513 it was decided that a new defence was needed. Flodden Wall, as it was called, ran southwards from the castle across Grassmarket, then east to enclose Greyfriars and Kirk o'Field; it then turned north just short of the Pleasance and followed the boundary between Edinburgh and the Canongate, before turning west near the site where Waverley Station now stands to meet the waters of the Nor' Loch, which protected the city from the north. Its four heavily defended gateways were the West Port at the end of the Grassmarket; the Bristo Port; the Cowgate Port; and the Netherbow Port at the entrance to the Canongate. The last, with its great central tower, divided the Royal Mile in two, and the lower half, the Canongate, then lay outside the boundaries of the city. This was the way the canons of the abbey of Holyrood would pass up and down in their visits to the town, and so it became known as the Canons' Walk or Gait. The Flodden Wall served as the effective boundary of the town until the eighteenth century, when Edinburgh overflowed into the New Town.

Mary's welcome into Edinburgh on 22 August 1561 was a well planned affair, and no expense was spared in the city's determination to impress on her its pre-eminent position. Musicians played and the people lining the streets joined the procession as it made its way from the Netherbow Port up towards the castle. At the newly completed Tolbooth were four young women representing the Virtues, while the maidens chosen to adorn the Mercat Cross excited much admiration (especially, no doubt, after the Royal Party had passed on, when wine gushed freely from the cross's spouts). The more offensive of the schemes inspired by the Protestant zeal of the Congregation, such as setting fire to a model of a priest saying Mass, had been surpressed by the Earl of Huntly, as we have seen. Instead, children were schooled to present Mary with a Protestant Bible and Psalter, and one made a speech imploring her to abandon the Mass. These incidents aside, however, the ceremonies were lavish enough for Mary to be well pleased with her reception.

The townspeople were fond of diverting themselves with any form of public entertainment. In 1544 the district of Greenside (at the top of Leith Walk, north-west of Calton Hill, where the Edinburgh Playhouse stands today) had been chosen as the site for open-air performances of plays and concerts by the town's musicians. The tolerant nature of Mary's mother is recorded in the fact that she once sat for nine hours on the bank of the hill to watch a performance of *The Pleasant Satire* by Sir David Lyndsay.

More boisterous entertainment was provided on Mayday every year when the town erupted in a carnival surrounding a play about Robin Hood and Little John, a free-for-all which was condemned by the more sober elements in the town as resulting in coarse, unseemly behaviour. Her mother having failed to ban the proceedings, Mary herself attempted to do so in 1562, claiming that they led to 'perturbation of the common tranquillity, wherein our good subjects are desirous to live'. Tradition proved hard to break, however, and even the disapproval of the Reformed church failed to dampen popular enthusiasm for this annual sport.

Much of the original layout of the Royal Mile is unchanged from four centuries ago, and areas with names like the Lawnmarket, the Grassmarket and the Cowgate bear witness to the kind of scenes that were their everyday events. There are two buildings, however, which remind us particularly of Mary's reign, above all in relation to her long tussle with that dour architect of the Scottish Reformation, John Knox.

Midway between the castle and the Netherbow, on a spot where a place of worship has existed since the middle of the ninth century, stands St Giles, the principal church of Edinburgh, at once pulpit and political platform for Knox. From the outside its most notable feature is its 'crown of stone', the lantern tower decorated with fretted pinnacles which stands high above the houses of the Old Town and can be seen from all over the city. The church was originally dedicated to the French 'Guid Sainct Geille' and belonged to the monastery of Lindisfarne. By the sixteenth century it had been rebuilt, enlarged, and endowed by the various trade guilds in Edinburgh until it took the shape of the magnificent

ABOVE *A sixteenth-century map of Edinburgh.*

BELOW *St Giles Cathedral,*
*Edinburgh's principal church.*

structure we know today. It was raised from the position of being an ordinary parish church in the middle of the fifteenth century to become a collegiate church with almost the status of a cathedral.

In the summer of 1559 Mary of Guise had posted a guard of sixty armed men around St Giles, and for further protection against the Lords of the Congregation and their campaign to clear all vestiges of popery from houses of worship, the crucifixes, candlesticks and altar furnishings were removed and hidden. Some of the altars were pulled down by the Protestants, but with the arrival of French troops to support Mary of Guise the old ceremonies were resumed. After 1560, however, with Mary dead and her troops defeated, the purging of idolatry from this old church was renewed with a vengeance. With the aid of ropes and ladders the carvings were splintered from the walls, and the ornaments and hangings were removed. When only the bare walls were left the whole interior was whitewashed. For the next twelve years Knox was the principal preacher.

John Knox was born at Gifford in about 1514 and probably trained for the priesthood at St Andrews University, becoming a priest by 1540. He was deeply influenced by the gentle Protestant preacher George Wishart, who was burned at the stake by Cardinal Beaton in 1546. Just over a year later Knox joined the Protestants who had subsequently murdered Beaton and occupied the castle. During this time he emerged as the spokesman of the Reformation movement. In June 1547 the castle was besieged and captured by Scottish and French troops, and Knox was taken prisoner and sent to France as a galley slave. Some two years later he was released, in response to English pressure, and spent several years preaching in England until Mary Tudor's accession in 1553 forced him to flee to the continent. Dismayed that the very existence of the reformed religion in England was so vulnerable to the personal beliefs of the monarch, Knox, after discussions with Calvin in Geneva, developed a more extreme form of Protestantism.

In 1559 Mary of Guise began to exert pressure on Protestant leaders in Scotland, who in response rallied their supporters and recalled Knox from Geneva. Edinburgh fell into Protestant hands, and Knox was elected minister of St Giles, where he continued to preach until his death. During the winter of that year the Lords of the Congregation fought a desperate battle against Mary's soldiers, and it was Knox's oratory as much as anything that sustained them until the spring, when Elizabeth at last sent English troops to their aid.

If Knox's early days were marked by severe hardship, his life in Edinburgh was one of comfort. His house in the High Street, given to him as a manse with its upkeep and furnishing provided for, is a well preserved example of a wealthy town house, and his salary of 400 Scots marks was generous for the time. But if one of the main reasons for the widespread popular support for his ideas had been the conspicuous extravagance of the Catholic church in the face of the poverty that the people themselves endured, by 1565 it was clear that their economic plight had not changed. The records of Edinburgh town council show that although a general poor tax was now imposed on all citizens, beggars were so numerous that officials were posted outside church doors to prevent their clamour from disturbing the services. Knox's plans for the improvement of education and poor relief had been abandoned for lack of finance after a scheme to endow the Reformed church with the Catholic church's wealth had failed.

After Mary took up residence at Holyrood she and Knox had a series of meetings which quickly became arguments, each one more impassioned and less polite than the last. Neither gave any ground, and the queen was sometimes left weeping with frustration. It was her misfortune that her principal opponent in the matter of religion and everything pertaining to it was both unyieldingly rigid and totally impervious to her charm, the weapon that she could always fall back on with more susceptible subjects.

*The house occupied by Knox is situated midway between the castle and the palace, in Edinburgh's Royal Mile.*

But if Knox drew a blank with his sovereign, he was at one time hopeful of success in persuading her young husband of the rightness of his cause, for in the August after the marriage Darnley attended a service at St Giles, hoping to ingratiate himself with the Protestants. Knox had no subtlety: he used the occasion to preach at length on the young man's duties as king. Darnley saw plenty of rights and privileges in the position – many of them relating to his hunting pursuits – but he seems to have had scant regard for the corresponding obligations of kingship. Nor was he the mental athlete who might have enjoyed the more circuitous parts of Knox's long discourse: by the end of the sermon he was 'extremely crabbit'.

Knox lived to see the ruin and imprisonment of the queen. In November 1572 he delivered his last sermon, so weak that his voice could barely be heard. On 24 November he

*The stately quadrangle of Edinburgh University covers the site of Kirk o' Field house, where, in February 1567, Mary's second husband, Lord Darnley, was murdered in circumstances that have never been explained.*

died and was buried in St Giles' churchyard, which is now covered by the Law Courts. His final resting place, now under the car park, is marked by a stone inscribed simply 'I.K.1572'.

By January 1566 it was certain that Mary was pregnant, and Darnley was creating public scandal with his drunken debauchery. On one occasion, when Mary attempted to curb his drinking at the home of an Edinburgh merchant, her remonstrations brought forth such abuse from Darnley that she left the house in tears.

On Thursday 7 March Mary, accompanied by Bothwell, Huntly and Crawford, attended a meeting of Parliament in the Tolbooth. This building, constructed in 1561 beside St Giles on the castle side, served as the council house for the collection of tolls, and was also the seat of the 'Session', and occasionally housed the Privy Council, the General Assembly of the Reformed church, and indeed Parliament. In later years it served as a prison and even as a place of public execution, with a gallows erected on a projecting roof. A heart-shaped arrangement of cobbles which used to mark its entrance led to it being referred to as the Heart of Midlothian. This particular meeting of Parliament fixed 12 March for the announcement of a bill against the Earl of Moray, who had opposed the marriage to Darnley, and the forfeiture of all his estates. The hand of the conspirators who supported Moray and the outlawed lords was now being forced.

Two days later the heavily pregnant queen was to witness the brutal murder of Rizzio. With the birth of her child now imminent Mary determined to conceal the true state of her marriage and a declaration of Darnley's innocence was read out at the Mercat Cross. This stood in the centre of the High Street close to the Tolbooth, where it had been in one shape or another since the founding of the burgh. Originally it represented the unity of the burgh, but by the sixteenth century its spiritual value had given way to more practical functions. It was used as a central meeting point where burgh laws were proclaimed and criminals punished and, standing out from the shade of the overhanging buildings, it also served as a handy drying place for clothes.

By the autumn of 1566 Darnley, aggrieved at what he felt to be the erosion of his status within the kingdom, announced his intention of leaving the country indefinitely. On Michaelmas Day he arrived at the gates of Holyrood but refused to enter until the noblemen then discussing affairs of state with Mary were dismissed; it was ten o'clock at night when Mary came out, dressed in her full regal attire, to try and dissuade him from this affront to her honour. After spending the night he stayed to attend a Privy Council meeting, but when questioned on his plans he simply jumped to his feet, exclaimed, 'Adieu Madame, you shall not see me for a long space,' and strode out of the palace for the last time.

By the new year he lay at his father's house in Glasgow, suffering from smallpox, or possibly the advanced stages of syphilis. On 20 January Mary set out to visit him and, knowing that he would be less of a threat away from the influence of his ambitious family, she persuaded him to return with her to Edinburgh; or, if the evidence of the casket letters is accepted as genuine, she lured him back to his destruction. She proposed that he lodge at Craigmillar Castle, but *en route* he raised objections to this, stating that he would prefer instead to convalesce at Kirk o'Field, on the outskirts of Edinburgh, where the Old College of Edinburgh University now stands. There he stayed in the house which had formerly been the lodging of the provost of St Mary's kirk. Mary visited him constantly, sitting with him there in the evenings and occasionally sleeping in one of the lower rooms. Tapestries and carpets were brought from Holyrood to furnish his apartments, and relations between the couple seemed peaceful. Violence was at hand, however, in thought if not yet in deed. Only seven days after Darnley's arrival, Paris, Mary's servant at Kirk o'Field, had obtained the keys of the house and turned them over to his old master, Bothwell. While Edinburgh watched Mary pass backwards and forwards by day, work secretly went ahead by night to fill the vaulted cellars of the house with gunpowder.

On Sunday 9 February two of Mary's favourite servants were married at Holyrood, and later there was a grand banquet in honour of the ambasssador from Savoy. Mary managed to excuse herself to visit her husband in the early evening and stayed chatting and playing dice until nearly eleven. Then she returned to Holyrood to put in an appearance at the wedding festivities. The dancing ended at twelve and Mary retired to bed. Two hours later Edinburgh was rocked by a tremendous explosion. Before long the whole of Edinburgh knew that Kirk o'Field had been reduced to rubble and the king in his nightgown lay dead in the garden. Beside him lay his servant, Taylor, and both bodies were unmarked: having escaped through a window before the explosion, king and servant had been caught and strangled as they fled.

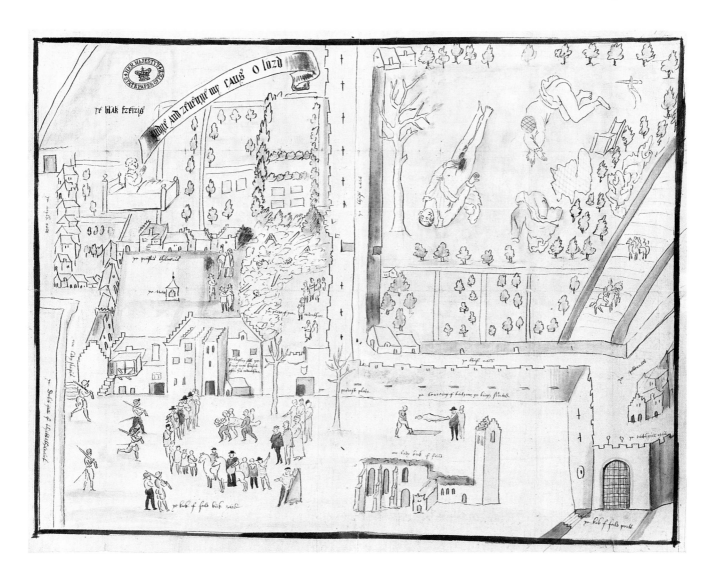

*A contemporary sketch of the murder. The question mark hanging over Mary's implication in the crime accounts for the enigma that follows her through the centuries.*

Darnley's corpse was brought to Holyrood, where it was embalmed and laid in state before the chapel altar. After a private ceremony it was then buried next to James v in the royal vault. If Mary herself was slow to grasp the true nature of events and too cast down to attempt to bring the assassins to justice, the people of Edinburgh were not too slow to point the finger. Placards appeared in the streets naming Bothwell and offering evidence, and as time passed and steps were still not taken to secure his arrest suspicion grew that Mary herself was implicated. The most damning placard appeared on 1 March, showing a crowned mermaid above a hare surrounded by swords. The hare was Bothwell's family crest, while the mermaid was a common euphemism for a prostitute. The significance was clear.

Yet Mary seemed incapable of acting to clear her name, and it was Lennox, Darnley's father, who finally forced the trial of Bothwell. It was to take place on 12 April, but on that day, with Bothwell and 4,000 supporters roaming the streets of the town, Lennox feared to enter the town gates. In the absence of the accuser, Bothwell was declared innocent. Not content with his acquittal, at a supper party in a public house called Ainslie's Tavern Bothwell persuaded other leading nobles – by drink, intimidation, or force of character – to support his suit for the queen's hand, in spite of the fact that he was still married to Lady Jean Gordon. If Mary's testimony is to be believed she rejected his first marriage proposal:

but Bothwell was above all a man of action. This was a quality which had worked to her advantage before: now it was to prompt a deed which was to prove another milestone on her road to disaster.

On 21 April, returning from a visit to the infant Prince James at Stirling, Mary was intercepted by Bothwell and escorted to Dunbar Castle, of which he had been made keeper after Rizzio's murder. Again, what actually happened must be left to individual conviction about the authenticity of the casket letters: either this was a pre-arranged tryst, the sequel to the queen's complicity in Darnley's murder, or it was a squalid abduction culminating in rape. On 6 May the couple returned to Edinburgh: Bothwell, the recipient of what must surely be one of the speediest divorces in history, walked bareheaded into the city as the queen rode, but he led her horse by the bridle. Three days later the banns of their marriage were proclaimed in St Giles by the personal order of the queen. In spite of widespread disgust at such unseemly haste, on 15 May Mary married Bothwell in a Protestant service in the chapel used as the Canongate church in Holyrood. This time there were no ostentatious celebrations, no goodwill gifts, and Mary was certainly in no mood for dancing. For three weeks Mary and Bothwell stayed at Holyrood, but the merry days of court life at the palace were long gone. Mary was suicidal as the folly of her marriage became daily more apparent: there was no reconciliation with the Scottish lords, and Bothwell refused them audience with the queen except in his presence. His behaviour towards Mary was contemptuous and he posted armed men at the doors of her rooms. On 6 June, hearing that a number of nobles were gathering their forces to march on Edinburgh, Bothwell removed Mary to Borthwick Castle, about twelve miles south of the city.

Just over a week later, after her surrender to the confederate lords on Carberry Hill, Mary returned to Edinburgh for the last time. Now there were no fountains flowing with wine but only jeers and accusations as she passed through the streets, her red petticoat splattered with mud and her cheeks stained with tears. She was taken to the Black Turnpike, the provost's house in the High Street, where she was confined for the night. Utterly humiliated, deserted and without comfort, Mary broke down. At daylight the crowds who gathered in the streets witnessed their queen leaning from her window, hysterical, her hair in tangles and her clothes unfastened. Her cries and accusations of treachery were met with insults. That evening she was conducted down to Holyrood with the Blue Blanket, the famous flag and historic rallying point of Edinburgh craftsmen, carried before her in protection against the mob. Its inscription must have seemed cruelly ironic:

> Fear God and honour the King
> With a long life, and prosperous reign,
> And we, the trades, shall ever pray
> For the defence of His Sacred Majesty's
> Person till death.

She was allowed only a few hours respite at the palace where, in the bright early years of her reign, the French and Scottish courtiers had created a brave imitation of the life she had known in France, and which until the horrific events of February 1566 stained its happiness for her was probably the favourite of all her Scottish residences. The palace was then a fairly recent building, erected close to the site of Holyrood Abbey. The abbey was founded in 1128, and its origins are steeped in legend. The most popular one is that on the day of the Holy Rood King David I announced his intention to amuse himself with a hunt in the lands below Edinburgh Castle. In spite of the entreaties of his confessor that the day be spent in prayer the hunt went ahead, and in the heat of the chase the king was thrown from his horse and found himself alone and about to be gored by an angry stag. As he gave himself up for

*Holyrood's most glittering, romantic and dramatic occasions took place when Mary held court there.*

lost a miraculous mist shrouded him and, putting out a hand to protect himself, he grasped a cross between the stag's antlers, and the stag took to flight. That night he dreamed that this was a divine command to found an Augustinian monastery upon the spot, and thus the abbey of Holyrood was endowed. A more reliable explanation of the abbey's origins lies in the claim that King David's mother, Queen Margaret, founded it as a repository for her fragment of the true Cross.

After fifty years of building the high abbey wall enclosed the abbey church with its great towers, a guest house and infirmary, a brewhouse, the abbot's house and stables, dormitories, refectories and vegetable and herb gardens. The canons were rich, with revenues from all over Scotland, and their lands included the burghs of the Canongate, Arthur's Seat and Restalrig.

The abbey was also granted rights of sanctuary which persisted, for debtors at least, until the beginning of this century. The boundary of the sanctuary lay at the foot of the Royal Mile where stood the Girth Cross (which seems to have served roughly the same purpose as the Mercat Cross in Edinburgh), and is now marked by a raised circle of cobbles. Behind Holyrood it extended over the whole area of Holyrood Park. There are many reports of debtors fleeing down the High Street, their furious creditors close on their heels, and leaping into sanctuary just in time. They were housed in the Abbey Strand, and these 'Abbey Lairds' ventured abroad only on Sundays.

The palace of Holyrood was built by James IV, who wanted it to be ready for his bride, Margaret Tudor, in 1503. The abbey, which owing to the abbots' policy of appeasement survived countless English invasions, was finally destroyed in the 'rough wooing'. In 1544 it was burned and looted and its brazen font was carried off gleefully to England, and in 1547 it was further destroyed and never afterwards wholly repaired. Much work was carried out on the palace meanwhile, however, and soon it was structurally sound if not ornately decorated. It was rather forbidding inside, too, for the thick walls and deep-set windows made the rooms gloomy and cheerless.

On 19 August 1561 the procession bearing Mary from Leith arrived at the gates of the palace, where the somewhat close and airless apartments had been brightened with candelabra and colourful trappings. Her rooms lay on the second floor and consisted of an audience chamber, bedroom, supper room and dressing room. In the audience chamber, where John Knox was later to be so outspoken, the ceiling was decorated with sixteen panels representing the alliance with France and depicting the arms of Mary's parents and of her late husband the dauphin as well as her own.

On the night of her arrival she was serenaded with psalms by some of the worthies of Edinburgh, who accompanied themselves on the bagpipes: the fastidious poet and gossip Brantôme, who formed part of the French retinue, found their efforts cacophonous and unbearable, but it must be said that his accounts were always laced both with French élitism and with enough malice to make them entertaining reading. Mary herself seems to have been touched by the tribute, and gallantly invited the musicians to return on subsequent nights.

For three and a half years she presided over banquets, masques, wedding feasts and other festivities from Holyrood. It was the most glittering time in the whole history of the palace. The nearby kirk of the Canongate was favoured by Protestant nobles for marriages, and if Mary's scruples forbade her to attend such occasions (though in time she herself was married there, by Protestant rites, to Bothwell), then she was all the more enthusiastic on the safe ground of the secular rejoicings afterwards.

Nor did she always remain within the relative formality of the palace bounds: from time to time she and her Maries would dress as merchants' wives and wander the streets of

Edinburgh. Her disguise seems to have been less successful than that of her father, who used to dress up as a commoner, but such behaviour never failed to incur the wrath of the easily scandalized Knox.

Yet the glitter of Mary's court was strangely lacking in substance. James IV had built Holyrood: his son added to it and embellished it until it was a magnificent Renaissance palace; and Mary's great-grandson Charles II endowed it with the gracious symmetry we see today. Mary's only physical legacy – indeed, perhaps the only building in Scotland directly attributable to her initiative – is the bath house that stands a little way away from what in her day was the north side of the palace.

There were no poets' 'flytings' as there had been in her father's day, and her days of splendour left no testament of poetry, drama or prose. Music was more receptive than literature to the strong French influence and some of that inheritance survives today, revived by increasingly popular early music groups. In their melodies we can find perhaps the strongest evocation of the atmosphere of Mary's court. Amongst the songs and airs that survive are some by the most famous musician of Holyrood, whose manner of death, however, is infinitely better known than his compositions.

The story is that Rizzio had come across to Scotland in the retinue of Signor de Moretta, the Savoyard ambassador. His rich voice was noticed by Mary, who needed a bass to make up her quartet. She asked him to leave Moretta's service and enter her own; he did so, and was soon her private secretary. The whole history of Rizzio's rise is generally related in a way that casts a sympathetic light on Mary, a lonely queen isolated amongst rough Scots nobles, needing the companionship of a civilized European who would have only her interests at heart. This view sees the jealousy of those nobles as wholly unjustified, and yet another example of their unbridled ambition. But there is another way of looking at the affair, which makes it clear that Mary's promotion of Rizzio was at best tactless and at worst showed complete lack of judgement in handling the affairs of her country.

Since she had arrived in Scotland her interests had been well served by two men above all: her brother, Moray, and her secretary of state, Maitland of Lethington. The two made a formidable alliance, united in purpose if differing in style: 'The Lord James dealeth according to his nature, rudely, homely, and bluntly; the Laird of Lethington more delicately and finely, yet nothing swerveth from the other in mind and effect', reported Randolph. They were skilful and sophisticated politicians, who had guided Mary's dealings with Elizabeth and the mighty Cecil, Maitland's opposite number. They had negotiated tirelessly, though fruitlessly, for the second marriage that she longed for, one to match her first in prestige. (The enthusiasm with which Mary herself promoted the idea of a foreign marriage, incidentally, shows her to have had a very limited commitment to a future in Scotland.) Moray and Lethington were also of particular assistance in helping her to avoid an open breach with Knox, and at the same time the former had managed to protect her own freedom of worship.

Fatally, she pushed aside men such as these, men who knew the political reality in Scotland as well as they knew the streets of Edinburgh, and relied instead on the readily sympathetic – possibly sycophantic – Rizzio. No wonder that he was resented, and the fact that he was so much in her confidence led to suspicions that together they were conducting secret negotiations with the pope. It is strange that it is the behaviour of Moray and Lethington that is so often called into account nowadays, while Rizzio is credited with disinterested loyalty, not ambition.

Most importantly, he was the last person to advise her in the question of marriage. Here, above all, she needed Moray's counsel – and his restraining influence. Instead, encouraged by Rizzio, she pushed ahead willy-nilly with the match that was to undermine everything

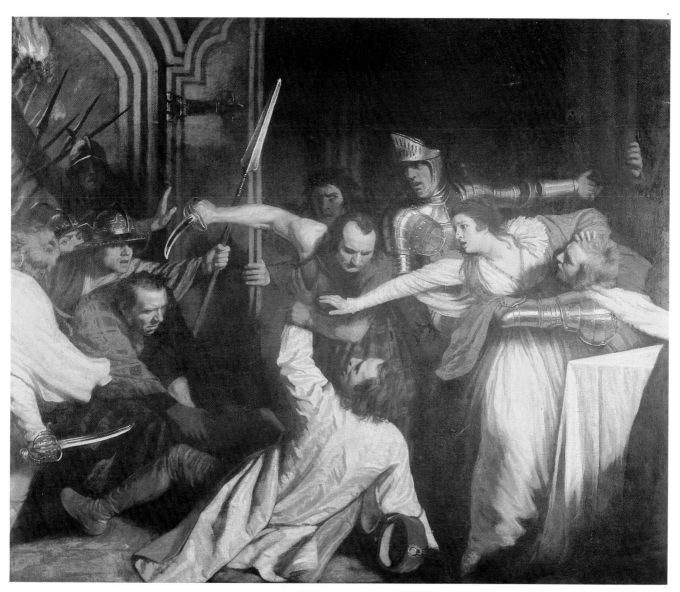

RIGHT *The Italian musician, David Rizzio, whose rise to influence as her personal secretary occasioned suspicion and jealousy from Mary's nobles. His horrific murder in her presence, in May 1566, exposed their treachery and that of her husband.*

ABOVE *The scene of Rizzio's murder, as depicted by John Opie. He was despatched with over fifty stab wounds.*

*Queen Mary's bath house at Holyrood. Is this the only testament in stone and mortar to her reign?*

that she had achieved in the four years since she had arrived back in Scotland, and which soured forever her relations with Moray, the man who had helped her to build that edifice. At the end of July 1565 she married Darnley in the chapel at Holyrood. Randolph despatched details of the occasion to the Earl of Leicester (who had himself once been put forward as a suitor) in London:

The manner of the marriage was of this sort. Upon Sunday, in the morning, between five and six, she was conveyed by diverse of her nobles to the chapel. She had upon her back the great mourning gown of black, with the great wide mourning hood, not unlike unto that which she wore the doleful day of the burial of her husband . . . The words were spoken, the rings, which were three, the middle a rich diamond, were put upon her finger, they kneel together, and many prayers said over them.

Within a very short time it was obvious that she had made a terrible mistake, for the nineteen-year-old Darnley was prepared to enjoy every available form of vice, to humiliate his wife publicly, to arouse the hostility of every noble, and to indulge in treachery when he thought it advantageous. He turned against Rizzio, and allowed himself to be seduced into taking part in the plot to murder the Italian in the presence of the seven-months' pregnant queen. He was gullible enough to be stirred to sexual jealousy, and was even suspicious as to the paternity of the child she was carrying. To the queen the plot could mean only one thing: the horror of seeing her favourite butchered by a large party of armed men, including her husband, was intended to bring on a miscarriage, with all its attendant dangers.

Mary herself described the brutal scene in a letter to the Archbishop of Glasgow, her ambassador in Paris. She had been at supper in a private upstairs apartment of the palace, next to her bedchamber. The room is remarkably small, and the spot where the murder took place is marked today by a brass plate in the wood floor. There were only half a dozen people around the table, including her half-sister and half-brother, her equerry, her page and Rizzio, wearing a gown of furred damask, a satin doublet and red velvet hose.

In the middle of supper, Darnley suddenly appeared at the head of the narrow stairway leading into the apartment, closely followed by the sickly Patrick, Lord Ruthven complete with steel helmet and armour. They demanded that Rizzio come with them; the queen protested and Rizzio cowered in the window recess of the tiny room. Ruthven denounced him and then lunged at him, shouting for his five followers, who rushed from their place on the staircase into the room. In a scene of frenzied savagery the supper table was overturned, while Rizzio clawed in vain at the queen's skirts. Although two of the attackers brandished pistols, the secretary was stabbed and hacked to death, screaming in French for his mistress to save him. There were between fifty and sixty wounds on his body, the first blow being struck by George Douglas using Darnley's own dagger. They dragged the torn and bleeding corpse down the stairs and left it lying across a wooden chest by the door.

Mary's behaviour at this juncture marks the high point of her behaviour during her reign. Overcoming her horror of him, she managed to subvert Darnley back to allegiance to her by playing on his fear of the lords; then she arranged their flight first to Seton and then to Dunbar. Moray, who was undoubtedly implicated in the plot at long distance, had returned from the exile she had imposed after his rebellion against her at the time of her marriage; but she used the occasion to effect a reconciliation of sorts. And she saved her baby. She returned to Edinburgh in triumph from Dunbar, but Holyrood had lost its charm for her forever. And from then on her periods of residence, brief as they were, coincided with further calamitous events: the night of the explosion at Kirk o'Field and the murder of Darnley; and the unhappy weeks of that brief and even more self-destructive third marriage.

Of all the royal palaces of the Scottish monarchs, Holyrood is the only one that remains a living focus of royal pageantry and hospitality. It was favoured by the later Stuart monarchs, though James VI only returned once after he had hot-footed it to London in pursuit of the crown of England. In the eighteenth century it again glittered with the temporary triumph of that other French-raised Stuart who tried and failed to establish Catholicism in a country which did not want it: Bonnie Prince Charlie.

It was through the imagination of Sir Walter Scott, who masterminded George IV's visit to Scotland in 1822, that an illusion of so much of the old Scotland bloomed again, albeit only on the short northern visits of monarchs whose responsibilities extended not just to Britain but to the vast territories of the empire. From the time of George IV's visit, Holyrood Palace has again been used regularly by Britain's kings and queens, and at banquets and receptions it might – just – be recognizable to the ghosts of Mary Stuart's court.

# 7

# FIFE: PLAYGROUND
# OF ROYALTY

OPPOSITE *The exquisite Falkland Palace, heart of James V's court and the scene of his death one week after his daughter's birth.*

BELOW *James V's coat of arms at Falkland.*

After a short stay in the capital, Mary embarked on a 'progress' of her kingdom. In fact she covered an extremely limited area, presumably that which was considered safest. She penetrated no further north than Perth, and no further west than Stirling, and the main thrust of her progress was around that kingdom within a kingdom, Fife. *En route*, however, she visited Dundee, then a small and relatively unimportant town, and there she left one of the few tangible testaments to her reign. Shocked by the people's primitive methods of disposing of their dead, she granted to the town the land which became the graveyard known as the Howff.

In Fife she was in a part of Scotland which had long associations with the royal house, and with her parents in particular. It was at the little fishing port of Crail that Mary of Guise first stepped on Scottish soil, and it was at St Andrews that she married James V and began her long commitment to her adopted country. It was to the little abbey of Balmerino on the Firth of Tay that James's first wife, the frail princess Madeleine, had gone in the fruitless hope that the therapeutic air there – and perhaps the skill of the monks – could stay the illness that would cause her death only a few weeks after her arrival in Scotland. But above all, for James V Fife was the county which contained his beloved Falkland, the palace which he completed and embellished until it became an exquisite, small-scale rival to the Renaissance châteaux of France. It can justifiably claim a place among the best Renaissance architecture, not just in Scotland but throughout Britain.

The palace and the little unspoiled town that surrounds it lie beneath the Lomond hills. There was a tower there from at least the thirteenth century, and within its walls, in 1401, the young Duke of Rothesay, heir to King Robert III, was starved to death by his ambitious uncle, Albany. There are stories of how the local people tried to help him: one relates how a miller's wife trickled grain through a crack in the prison wall, another how a nursing mother expressed her milk into his cell through a straw.

It was thirty-six years later that Falkland was appropriated by the crown, and from then on there were numerous repairs and additions to the tower. James V had spent parts of his guarded boyhood at Falkland, and it was from there in 1528 that he slipped away from the Douglases and galloped through the dawn towards Stirling and freedom. Shortly afterwards he started work on the new palace, slightly away from the original site. The French character of Falkland's architecture is frequently attributed to the influence of James's wives, but since the building was begun as early as 1530, at a time when he was more concerned with his Scottish mistresses, it must owe more to the French workmen he employed. But the finishing touches were put to this lovely palace after Mary of Guise became queen in 1540, and they commemorate the marriage.

Falkland was the focal point of James's court: a centre for the arts and a base from which to indulge his passion for hawking and hunting in the forests of Fife – in those, that is, that had not been felled by his father for the sake of building up the Scottish navy. Falkland was

*Hic pudor, hic morum probitas hic aulica fuada, Et lepor, & vitæ generofa modeftia qlifcit. Quid mirum, divas vltrò fi dià fequantur.*

the base from which he made his way, dressed as a commoner, to mingle unidentified amongst his subjects and to pursue his amorous conquests. It was to Falkland that he came, like a wounded animal retreating to its lair, to give up the effort of living after the humiliating disaster of Solway Moss. And here, on his deathbed, he heard the news of the birth of his daughter. He must have known that his end was near: and with the memory fresh in his mind of the death the previous year of his two sons by Mary of Guise, he can have held out little hope for the survival beyond infancy of the new child. In a phrase that subsequently became famous, he observed that the royal house of Stewart had 'cam wi' a lass, and will gang wi' a lass'. He did indeed accurately predict their eventual eclipse with a female of the line, but it was Queen Anne, not Queen Mary, who in the early eighteenth century was to be the last Stuart monarch of the line that had succeeded to the throne through the daughter of Robert the Bruce.

In time Falkland became a favourite of James's daughter as well, and she stayed there many times during her six years of personal rule. Her visits seem to have been untroubled, with the emphasis on sporting pleasures. There was even a tennis court, built for James in 1539, which still survives, unique in Scotland. Day-to-day management was in the hands of a captain or keeper, a hereditary office which in the sixteenth century was vested in the family of Mary Beaton. In the last century, the sad decay of the once magnificent palace was halted by its keepers of the Crichton-Stuart family, and now, most appropriately, the keeper is the National Trust for Scotland.

But above all it was St Andrews, home of Scotland's oldest university, that drew Mary again and again to Fife. Judging by the number and length of her visits there, this must have been one of her favourite parts of the kingdom. There was a palace in St Andrews, but it was an episcopal and not a royal one – the seat of the Primate of Scotland. And in the years of Mary's nonage, especially just before her departure for France, it was this status, coupled with the fact that its incumbent at the time was Cardinal David Beaton, that made it the setting for some of the most crucial events leading up to the Reformation. They began with the immolation before its walls of one of the chief prophets of that movement in Scotland, George Wishart. A wandering evangelist, he preached to receptive congregations throughout the east of Scotland, spreading the word of the new religion, the influence of which was already felt in this area through trade with northern, Lutheran, Europe.

OPPOSITE *On her first royal progress Mary granted the burgesses of Dundee the land known as the Howff, for use as a graveyard.*

TOP AND BELOW *Two forms of sixteenth-century Scottish dancing: the formalized court measures, and the more uninhibited dances of the peasantry.*

*Quantum aula à Caula tantum quoq diftat agrefti. Aulicus: hoc præfens te laxa Chorea docebit. Sed bene, fic variæ liquæant difcrimina vitæ.*

Wishart was not like his ranting and iconoclastic successor, John Knox. He was described as a man 'of great knowledge, of pleasant utterance, humble, modest, charitable and patient'. Undeterred by the anti-reformist legislation, he continued his preaching unmolested until 1545. Then, on a visit to Haddington, Wishart was apprehended by Patrick, Earl of Bothwell in his capacity as Sheriff of Haddington. Despite apparently giving the preacher assurances of safety, Bothwell delivered him to Beaton. Wishart stood trial for heresy in February 1546, and in March, with great courage, died at the stake. As usual, repression inflamed rather than dampened the fires of revolution. Wishart's valedictory request to lay aside rancour, envy and vengeance did not reach the ears of his followers. Vengeance swiftly followed martyrdom.

*The Protestant martyr George Wishart, burned for heresy before the walls of St Andrews Castle.*

St Andrews Castle is now a ruined shell, half swept away by the sea. But in 1546 it was in its full glory. It had not shared the fate of the Border Abbeys and many other closer establishments, and was still a treasure house of precious metals and stones, of elaborate carvings and richly embroidered episcopal vestments, of charters, missals, and illuminated manuscripts. It was in all probability far richer than any of the royal palaces. The grand banqueting hall where Beaton held sumptuous court lies on the ocean bed now, but the remains of his private chamber with its communicating door into the chapel may still be seen. So too may the bottle-shaped dungeon from which there was no exit.

The conspirators whose plotting was to culminate in Beaton's death were led by Norman Leslie, son of the Earl of Rothes, and 'the young Laird of Grange', Sir William Kirkcaldy, who was to play so crucial a part in Mary's reign. It has been suggested that the conspiracy against Beaton pre-dated Wishart's death, and the martyr's own prophecy that the cardinal, who was a spectator at his immolation, would shortly follow him to supreme judgement, is cited as evidence of Wishart's own complicity. Given his gentle character, this seems unlikely. However, in May 1546 work was being carried out to improve the defences of the castle: Beaton was obviously uneasy. As the gates opened before dawn on 29 May to admit the early-morning contingent of masons and joiners, the conspirators mingled with the workmen. The gatekeeper recognized John Leslie of Parkhill and attempted to raise the drawbridge, but for his vigilance was murdered and thrown into the moat.

Beaton quickly realized what was happening. Seizing his two-handed sword (he was versed in the arts of war as well as of statecraft) he retreated to his own room and, with the help of a servant, barricaded himself in. John Leslie called for a fire to burn down the door: it was brought 'in ane chumlay'. In the horrific spectacle which the scene must have presented – the great cardinal cowering, trapped and stripped of all semblance of power, clothed not in his splendid vestments but in a nightgown and with only a few minutes to live – the incongruity of the fire in the chamberpot strikes a note of farce. Through the barricade Beaton tried to bargain for his life. His end was much less dignified than that of the man he had condemned a few months previously: 'I am a priest, I am a priest, ye will not slay me,' he begged, but no fewer than three of the invaders joined in his final despatch.

*The distinctive bottle dungeon at St Andrews Castle, said by some sources to have held Beaton's salted corpse for several months.*

His body suffered manifold indignities: stripped of the tattered remnants of his nightgear it was exhibited to the crowd of townsfolk who had gathered outside the castle. Sources differ as to whether the corpse was naked or arrayed in its episcopal glory, and whether it was thrown into the castle dungeon or a midden: Sir David Lyndsay takes the latter option in his poem 'The Tragedy of the Cardinal':

> I lay unburyit for seven monthis and more
> Or I was borne to cloister, kirk or queir,
> In ane mydding, whilk paine bene tyll deplore
> Without suffrage of chanoun, monk or frere.

DAVID BETONIVS · S · R · E · CARD · ARCHIEP · S · ANDRÆ
IN SCOTIA AB HOSTIBVS FIDEI BARBARE TRVCIDATVS

*Cardinal Beaton, principal adviser to both James V and his widow Mary of Guise. His murder in 1546 was in direct retaliation for Wishart's execution.*

What is undisputed is that the body was salted like a side of beef. Though there is no comparison between the status and power of the two victims, in personal terms there is a hideous parallel between the murder of Beaton at St Andrews and that of Rizzio at Holyrood thirty years later. The latter was, if anything, the more horrific crime: the victim was certainly innocent of the shedding of others' blood, and was brutally cut down in the presence of the pregnant queen. But the consequence for Mary of Guise was the same as it was twenty years later for her daughter: she was bereft of her most trusted adviser. Though the queen mother was infinitely shrewder, more capable and tougher than her daughter, she must now have felt desperately isolated. She was also increasingly vulnerable to criticism and resentment from both the pro-English and the pro-French factions among the lords, for now the francophile policy, rather than being in the hands of one who believed it to be in the interests of his own country, was instead controlled by a native Frenchwoman.

As also with Mary and Rizzio, there had been hints at a deeper relationship between Mary and Beaton than that of mere political allies. Sir Ralph Sadler, that ever-assiduous bearer of gossip, relates that 'in the late king's time he had her in some jealousy for over familiarity betwixt her and the cardinal'. Then there is the unreliable testimony, in 1565, of a dismissed page to James Hepburn, Earl of Bothwell, who related that his master had stated of Queen Mary, that 'if she had taken with any but a cardinal, it had better to be borne with'. To which queen did this apply?

After Beaton's murder his assassins occupied the castle at St Andrews, where they were joined by other dissidents, including John Cockburn of Ormiston and John Knox. Known as the 'castilians', they became a focus of protest against the Catholic church and the accompanying pro-French policy. What started as an occupation became a siege, and eventually, in July 1547, eight French ships appeared off the coast of Fife. Two were 'great ships' and six were galleys, manned by slaves whose complement would in due course be swelled by some of the captured castilians. Knox, never a reliable chronicler of events from which he could draw political advantage, stated that 'a good fight was made' and a galley sunk through the efforts of the garrison; but it seems more likely that the ship was grounded through bad navigation. The French landed and under the captaincy of the Prior of Capua mounted guns in the college and the abbey and bombarded the castle. The castilians, forced to surrender, were transported in the galleys to France: it was eleven years before Knox was to reappear in Scotland, bringing with him the accumulated resentment of years against the Catholic church in Scotland and its supporters of the royal house; and bringing too the evangelical zeal of the Calvinist doctrines he had imbibed in Geneva. By the time Mary visited St Andrews, it was Knox's brand of religion that was paramount in Scotland.

Her brother, Lord James Stewart, in spite of being one of Knox's adherents, was not averse to retaining the office arranged for him by his father, commendator (lay abbot) of the abbey of St Andrews, nor to deriving a considerable income from its revenues. On Mary's first visit on her progress she probably accepted Lord James's hospitality at the house attached to his office there. On later visits the house of his chamberlain, David Orme, was put at the queen's disposal. Orme had built up substantial holdings in that part of the town nearest to the abbey, and according to tradition the house in which she stayed had belonged

*A view of St Andrews Castle, the episcopal seat of the Primate of Scotland. After Beaton's death it was occupied by supporters of the Reformation until its capture by French troops.*

*The home in South Street, St Andrews, which Mary occupied in simplicity and happiness on several occasions.*

to that wealthy middle-class gentleman. It still stands in South Street, and the rooms where Mary once discoursed in Latin with George Buchanan are now used as the library of St Leonard's School, Scotland's leading independent girls' school. But even her days in St Andrews were not altogether unclouded. On her first long visit there, in the spring of 1562, news was brought to her of the supposed plot to kidnap her by Arran and Bothwell. Summoned to St Andrews, Bothwell was briefly lodged in the castle before being taken to Edinburgh.

If this episode had been embarrassing, however, the one in which she was involved immediately before her visit to St Andrews in the following year was considerably worse (though at least it did not involve her most prominent nobles), for it put her in a compromising position. Amongst the train that had followed her from France was the poet Pierre de Châtelard. Having returned to his own land with the main party, he then came back to Scotland, allegedly for love of the queen. Mary, then twenty, seems to have behaved with considerable naïvety, showing Châtelard special favour and even a certain physical familiarity: 'She would lie upon Châtelard's shoulder, and sometimes privily she would steal a kiss of his neck,' gossiped Knox excitedly. By her favouritism she offended many of her own nobles (a foretaste of the Rizzio affair), and there was worse to come.

On two separate occasions, and not at the invitation of the queen, Châtelard found his way into the royal bedroom. The first time, at Holyrood, the incident was hushed up: but the second importunity, on a visit to Burntisland in Fife, caused a commotion so great that Moray insisted that the matter be dealt with publicly (Mary had been quite prepared for her brother to despatch the would-be lover on the spot).

The queen went from Burntisland to St Andrews, and Châtelard followed to meet his execution. The poet made sure that the maximum drama was extracted from his death-scene: having recited Ronsard's 'Hymn to Death', he cried to the watching queen, 'O cruel dame!' Knox, seeking to invest the scene with as much moral import as possible, took these words to mean 'O cruel mistress', and dwelt on their ambiguity. Such, he added, was Châtelard's retribution for dancing.

That Mary was indiscreet, and to a minor extent brought scandal on herself, is indisputable. But there was some suspicion that Châtelard's return had been engineered by her enemies in France, and that his courtship of her and his attempts to compromise her were all a Machiavellian plot designed to frustrate the glittering second foreign marriage she

ABOVE *A contemporary plan showing the layout of sixteenth-century St Andrews.*

LEFT *Mary and her second husband, Darnley, whom she first met on a visit to Wemyss Castle in Fife.*

longed for. Not long after Châtelard's execution came another blow, from which her courtiers shielded her for as long as possible for fear of her reaction. In the end it was 'the wise Mary Beaton' who felt able to cope with breaking the news of the murder of her uncle, Duke Francis of Guise, by a Huguenot.

It is from Mary Beaton's admirer, the English ambassador Thomas Randolph, that we get the most charming description of the queen at St Andrews. Early in February 1565, Randolph had occasion to visit her there, and he reported what he found to Queen Elizabeth: 'Her grace lodged in a merchant's house; her train were very few; and there was small repair from any part. Her will was, that for the time that I did tarry, I should dine and sup with her. Your Majesty was oftentimes drunken unto by her, at dinners and suppers.' After a few days of this, Randolph felt it was high time for the matters that had brought him to St Andrews to be discussed, but:

I had no sooner spoken these words, than she saith, 'I see now well that you are weary of this company and treatment. I sent for you to be merry and to see how like a bourgeois wife I live, with my little troop; and you will interrupt our pastime with your great and grave matters. I pray you sir, if you be weary here, return home to Edinburgh, and keep your gravity and great ambassage until the queen come thither; for I assure you, you shall not get her here, nor I know not myself where she is become. You see neither cloth of estate, nor such appearances, that you may think there is a queen here; nor I would not that you should think that I am she, at St Andrews, that I was at Edinburgh.'

Randolph's 'great and grave matter' was his royal mistress's suggestion that Mary should marry Robert Dudley, Earl of Leicester, who had reputedly been Elizabeth's own lover. Not long after her meeting with Randolph, and still not having given him an answer, Mary went to Wemyss Castle, also in Fife, on her way back to Edinburgh. There, in the splendidly situated pink sandstone castle perched above the Firth of Forth, she met the young man for whose sake she was to turn all the success of the early years of her reign on its head: her cousin, Henry, Lord Darnley.

Darnley was the son of Matthew, Earl Lennox, and Margaret Douglas, the daughter of Margaret Tudor through her second marriage. He thus had claims to the succession of both the Scottish and English crowns, and he had already been put forward from time to time as a candidate for Mary's hand (the first occasion being when he was in his mid-teens and Mary newly widowed). Because he was reputed to have embraced Protestantism, this was a suggestion that appears to have carried some weight initially with Moray. But any advantage in Darnley's religion – and even in that he was ambivalent – was more than outweighed by his personal deficiencies. None of these were evident at first: he had grown up at the English court, and had an easy manner and a superficial charm. He also had considerable beauty, and was tall – he more than matched Mary in height – athletic and musical. Of Mary's potential second husbands, moreover, he was the only one who actually wooed her in person (other than the young Earl of Arran, whose lack of charisma was matched by his reforming zealotry, and who was also by now mad). But the gloss of Darnley masked corruption beneath. For his sake Mary broke with Moray, depriving herself of his experienced counsels, and defied the other leading nobles who also opposed the marriage, so encouraging an undercurrent of resentment against her. She married for love, or for lust, and probably persuaded herself that it was a suitable match. But in the end it proved that her rejected advisers knew better than she did.

She returned to Fife, to St Andrews and Falkland only rarely after marrying Darnley. From then on, despite brief plateaux of success, the pattern of events moved steadily towards disaster: precipitating them and accompanying her was the alcoholic, adulterous, overbearing and rather stupid youth to whom she had shackled herself. She had seen him at Wemyss as 'the properest and best-proportioned long man' that she had ever seen.

# 8

# THE NORTH:
# QUELLING AN UPRISING

One of the paradoxes of Mary's reign was that the first challenge to her authority came not, as might be expected, from a member of the Protestant faction among her lords, but from one of the leading Catholics. It was this challenge which prompted her most extensive progress to the northern regions – in both distance and length of time. It lasted from the second half of August 1562 until the early part of November of that year.

George Gordon, fourth Earl of Huntly, seems to have regarded himself for various reasons as the most significant of the Scottish nobles. Of those who shared the queen's religion he was indeed the premier in rank, and this should have been a binding link with her. In the early days after her arrival he certainly appointed himself as a kind of protector of the Catholic faith, as became evident when he stopped the more outspoken anti-papal pageants on her official reception in Edinburgh. But her realistic and pragmatic approach to the matter of religion – and politics – in Scotland was more than he could accept. Superficially at any rate, Mary was willing to accept the status quo, so long as she could guarantee freedom of worship for her Catholic subjects as well as herself. Huntly on the other hand wanted the new order overthrown as soon as possible and Catholicism restored by an armed *coup d'état* if necessary.

Huntly may also have considered that in a nation where many of his peers were relatively young men, his seniority in age should confer on him seniority in rank; and very likely he felt that his imposing physical stature was enough to assure him of moral and political authority too. Certainly he made no effort to render his large figure inconspicuous by sober dressing, even on the field of battle, where his white and gilt armour shone out for all to see. But the major reason why Huntly felt himself so pre-eminent and able to challenge Mary's authority was the power he wielded in the north-east, particularly in the important city of Aberdeen. Throughout the first months of her personal rule Mary's leading Catholic gradually estranged himself, when he should have been establishing his position in her favour. By June 1562, Cecil was able to deduce from reports he had received in London that 'In Scotland ... the Earl of Huntly is in no credit with the queen. The whole governance rests with Lord James, being Earl of Mar, and the Laird of Lethington. The others that are in favour are ... all Protestants.'

Two matters in particular led to the confrontation between Mary and Huntly in the autumn of that year. The ostensible reason was the behaviour of Huntly's son, Sir John Gordon, who was due to stand trial in Edinburgh. The details of his case were complicated and somewhat scandalous, and need not be related here; what was important was that Sir John openly defied the queen by escaping from custody and making for the Highlands. But there was another reason why it was necesssary at this juncture for the queen to challenge the power of the Gordons. At the time of Lord James Stewart's marriage at the beginning of the year, Mary had bestowed on her brother not just the earldom of Mar (soon to be resigned by him, and in the course of time transferred to its historical claimants, the Erskines) but also, secretly, the valuable earldom of Moray. This had not been made public because since 1549 Huntly had enjoyed the revenues although not the title of Moray.

Mary set out from Perth, a town of some importance which had once been a potential capital of Scotland and which had long and sometimes tragic associations with the rulers of Scotland. It was here that the first King James had been murdered by rebellious nobles in front of his wife, the first of the violent deaths that were to haunt generations of the house of Stewart. A mile or so from Perth, on the route Mary was to take to the east, is Scone, where Scottish kings had traditionally been crowned on the Stone of Scone. Since the invasion of Edward I that stone had been in Westminster Abbey, and Mary's son would be the first for many generations to be anointed sovereign – albeit of England – above it.

Perth was a leading centre of the Reformation. Not only were Mary's advisers of that faith, but the commanders of her army at that time were such men as Kirkcaldy of Grange and Cockburn of Ormiston, who had held St Andrews Castle against her mother's troops following the murder of Cardinal Beaton. The expedition to crush Huntly is often depicted – especially by novelists – as taking Mary through Highland fastnesses and remote glens peopled by the half-wild, Gaelic-speaking men and women of the north. In fact her journey took her across the rolling plains of Angus and up the eastern coastline, through countryside which could never be described as the Highlands. In a golden autumn the Angus farms yield up their agricultural riches with generosity, and the seaboard towns reap their own harvest of the seas. But it can be the coldest corner of Scotland, whipped by snell winds driving across the North Sea from the Russian steppes; and in the year of Mary's journey the driving rain and the chilly breezes were too much for some of the company, as were the distances between suitable castles. Randolph described the journey as 'cumbersome, painful, and marvellous long; the weather extreme foul and cold, all victuals marvellous dear; and the corn that [there] is, never like to come to ripeness.' The following year, according to Knox, was even worse: 'The year of God 1563, there was a universal dearth in Scotland. But in the Northland where, the harvest before, the queen had travelled, there was an extreme famine, in which many died in that country. The dearth was great all over, but the famine was principally there.' For Knox there was an explanation for such unseasonable weather. It was caused by the 'idolatory of our wicked queen'.

The first two castles at which she stayed after setting out from Perth are well worth visiting, though each has undergone dramatic changes since the autumn of 1562. Glamis was entirely restructured in the seventeenth century by Patrick, first Earl of Strathmore, whose trials and tribulations with his workmen (he complained of the 'shameless greed' of the masons) make interesting reading and strike a familiar note today. Later centuries have made their mark too, and the present fairy-tale castle, adjoined by the ancient and pretty village that shares its name, bears almost no resemblance to the castle that received the cold, tired cavalcade of Mary Queen of Scots. Glamis' association with royalty spans the centuries before and after Mary's reign. It is most famous for having been the seat of that much-maligned king, Macbeth, originally the Thane of Glamis. And in this century, it has seen the girlhood of Queen Elizabeth the Queen Mother and the birth of Princess Margaret. The centuries have domesticated Glamis, and today it is both a family home and a popular tourist attraction.

Edzell Castle, on the other hand, once the seat of the earls of Crawford and the largest castle in the county of Forfar, is now a solitary pink-stone ruin whose former grandeur may be guessed at from its imposing façade, which remains almost intact, and from its extensive foundations. In this it is of course similar to many Scottish castles of the period, but it has one special feature: the garden. Strictly speaking this belongs more to the time of Mary's son than to her own, but it is typical of the kind of garden that would have belonged to many of

OPPOSITE *After their joint expedition to the north-east, Mary made public her grant of the earldom of Moray to her brother James Stewart.*

BELOW *George Gordon, Earl of Huntly.*

the castles she visited during her reign. The garden at Edzell Castle is perhaps the most complete one of that period in the whole of Britain. In a slightly sunken area, formal rosebeds and lawns are surrounded by low box hedges which spell out Latin epigrams. They also form stylized patterns of the French fleur-de-lis, the Scottish thistle, the English rose and the Irish shamrock, making horticultural play on Mary's one-time dream of the united crowns. Looking down on the gardens from the ruined tower, it is easy to imagine Mary and her courtiers making their way across the lawns.

The progress went northwards, keeping to the coast through Stonehaven to Aberdeen, seat of what was then Scotland's youngest university. Huntly and his sons were nowhere to be found, and Lady Huntly's spirited and persistent intervention on their behalf was of no avail in pacifying the queen. Mary avoided making a detour to Huntly's own stronghold of Strathbogie, according to Randolph the 'largest and fairest' house in Scotland, and was wise to do so: amongst Huntly's wilder projects was one to detain her by force and impose on her a marriage with Sir John Gordon.

So she continued to Inverness, where the ultimate insult to her authority was delivered. The doors of Inverness Castle – which was a royal holding – were closed against her, the captain (Huntly's son, Alexander) preferring Huntly's authority to the queen's. But local feeling was in her favour, and only about a dozen men were left to hold the castle. It was surrendered, and in her treatment of Alexander Gordon Mary displayed none of the squeamishness with which she is often associated: he was hanged, and his head was put on public display.

But Huntly himself was still nowhere to be seen, and Mary retraced her steps to Spynie Palace, near Elgin. This was not a royal palace, but an episcopal one – the ruins of several such stand throughout Scotland – and was the residence of the Bishop of Moray. It may seem strange now that the palace was two and a half miles from the cathedral, but in fact Spynie was the original seat of the diocese. In 1224, however, the pope decreed that Elgin was a more suitable place, and that most exquisite of cathedrals, the 'Lamp of the North', was built in the town.

The solid keep that dominates the ruins of Spynie looks more appropriate to a fortress than to an ecclesiastical residence. It is said to have been built towards the end of the fifteenth century by Bishop David Stewart, who was at odds with the Earl of Huntly of his time. Having been threatened by the earl, who in his challenge also described the palace insultingly as 'pigeon holes', Bishop Stewart set about building a keep that would hold the earl and his clan at bay.

Bishop Hepburn, the incumbent of Mary's day, was a great-uncle of the Earl of Bothwell, who spent much of his youth at Spynie. His great-uncle seems to have had responsibility for the education of the boy, and perhaps set hardly the best example in terms of personal morality. True, the law of clerical celibacy was often flouted (Cardinal Beaton, for instance, kept a mistress and made provision for his children by her quite openly), but Bishop Hepburn carried things to excess: his children by several mothers were so numerous that he found himself duplicating names amongst them. Apologists for James Hepburn's profligacy with women lay the blame at the door of his episcopal great-uncle. But the bishop does seem to have had the merit of loyalty. He sheltered Bothwell when, five years later, the latter was hunted and outlawed and only a very few would still own him as an ally. Only a fight instigated by one of the bishop's many bastards drove Bothwell from Spynie and from the mainland of Scotland forever. Even during the long years of his great-nephew's subsequent imprisonment in Denmark, the Bishop of Moray continued to support his cause and press for his release until his own death in 1575.

At the time of writing visitors to Spynie are discouraged because of its dangerous state, though a clear view of it can be had from the road. But the extent of the renovations gives hope that in the future followers in Mary's Stuart's footsteps will be able to gain a clearer impression of the building where she spent some September days. And her spirits were high despite the vexation and worry that Huntly was causing, as Randolph, in an admiring mood, described in his despatch from Spynie: 'In all these broils I assure you I never saw her merrier, never dismayed, nor ever thought that stomach to be in her that I find. She repented nothing but . . . that she was not a man, to know what life it was to lie all night in the fields, or to walk on the causeway with a jack and knapsack, a Glasgow buckler and a broadsword.'

The opportunity for the use of broadswords and other weapons was soon to come. For nearly two months Huntly and Mary had played a game of cat-and-mouse. But confrontation could not be postponed forever: and when it came, on 28 October, on the field of Corrichie, the power of the Gordons was broken forever. Sir John and his younger brother Adam were taken prisoner and Sir John later executed; and Huntly himself fell dead of a stroke. For a few days debate raged about what should be done with the gross corpse: eventually it was disembowelled and taken to Edinburgh, where six months later it was arraigned for treason. This unpleasant custom was described in a contemporary manuscript:

The coffin was set upright, as if the Earl had stood on his feet, and upon it a piece of good black cloth with his [heraldic] arms fast pinned. His accusation being read, his proctor answering for him, as if himself had been alive, the inquest was empannelled. The verdict was given that he was found guilty,

*This wildly romantic painting claims to depict the battle of Carberry Hill. However, all the evidence points to its being a representation of Corrichie.*

and judgement given thereupon as by the law is accustomed. Immediately hereupon the good black cloth that hung over the coffin was taken away, and in its place a worse hanged on, the arms torn in pieces in the sight of the people, and likewise struck out of the herald's book.

So ended Mary's first and longest visit to the north. She returned once more to Inverness, and proceeded beyond it to Dingwall and to Beauly; but she never really penetrated inland into the heart of the Highlands, keeping instead to the relatively civilized east coast, with its abbeys and castles and its university. It was another two centuries before her descendant Prince Charles Edward Stuart launched his bid to re-establish a Catholic dynasty from that part of Scotland where the Reformation had taken least hold. And with his defeat the Highlands for the first time were opened up to easy access, and to the power of the south.

Huntly's heir, the fifth earl, was in time restored to his estates by Mary, and proved to be one of her most devoted lieutenants; a close ally, and for a time brother-in-law of Bothwell. The formidable dowager, too, was able to overcome any natural rancour following the deaths of her husband and sons, and served the queen with loyalty and resourcefulness. It was in part due to her presence of mind that Mary was able to make her escape from Holyrood after Rizzio's murder.

After the battle of Corrichie, it would be another six years before troops under Mary's command would engage an opposing army in battle. When this did happen, the rebel army would have at their head the man who was her closest ally in the northern campaign: her brother, who was now publicly declared Earl of Moray.

# 9

## THE MARIES:
## HOMES AND FAMILIES

*Creich Castle in Fife, built at the beginning of the sixteenth century. This was the seat of the branch of the influential Beaton family to which Mary Beaton belonged.*

The four young women who shared Mary's Christian name, her childhood, and above all her years in Scotland, act like a kind of chorus in her wake. Their identity should first be unravelled, to dispel the popular misconceptions which crop up in all kinds of unlikely areas, including the remarks of guides to buildings associated with the queen.

That one was Mary Beaton and one was Mary Seton generally causes no confusion. The names of Mary Hamilton and Mary Carmichael are sometimes linked with them, as in the popular ballad, 'The Queen's Maries', or alternatively 'The Ballad of Mary Hamilton', which has as its refrain the lines:

> Yestre'en the Queen had four Maries,
> The Nicht she'll hae but three,
> There was Mary Beaton, and Mary Seton,
> And Mary Carmichael, and me.

'Me' was the Mary Hamilton of the title, but the incident related in the ballad – the execution of a lady-in-waiting for the murder of her child by the king – has no foundation in the history of Mary Stuart's court: it happened in Russia, at the court of Peter the Great. The other two members of the famous four who graced the court of sixteenth-century Scotland were Mary Fleming and Mary Livingstone. They were carefully chosen, presumably by Mary of Guise, from families who had close connections both with the royal house of Stewart and with France.

*The Great Historic Families of Scotland*, a somewhat selective eighteenth-century compendium, says of the Seton family: 'The Setons are among the most illustrious of the great houses of Scotland, conspicuous throughout their whole history for their loyalty and firm attachment to the Stewart dynasty, in whose cause they perilled and lost their titles and extensive estates.' The family's founder, Secker de Seye, had been granted lands in East Lothian to which he gave his own name – Seytun, later Seton. His son acquired the estate of Winchburgh in West Lothian, and an early bearer of the name, Sir Christopher Seton, married the sister of Robert the Bruce. After heroic deeds in support of his brother-in-law's cause he was captured by English forces and executed at Dumfries. One of his brothers shared his fate, but a third lived through the wars to be a signatory of the Arbroath Declaration of Independence, and also a recipient of King Robert's gratitude towards the family. The existing Seton lands were enlarged by means of adding those confiscated from anglophile families, and a large stretch of the Lothian coastline became Seton territory.

The family continued to play a distinguished and colourful part in the developing history of Scotland, marrying into other noble families and from time to time into the fringes of royalty. Perhaps one of the most interesting members of the main line was the second Lord Seton, who seems to have been one of James IV's Renaissance men *par excellence*. Towards

the end of the fifteenth century he endowed a collegiate church in the small town that bears his name with support for a provost, six prebendaries, two choirboys and a clerk. He was an early scientist and is described as 'meikle given to leichery [medicine, not lustfulness], and as cunning in divers sciences as in music, theology, and astronomy'. Allied to this thirst for learning was an unbridled extravagance. He took to building houses as well as his church, and spent vast sums of money on buying a great ship called the *Eagle*, for the sole purpose of conducting a personal vendetta against some Danish privateers who had plundered him on one of several study visits to France.

As a result, his son, Mary Seton's grandfather, inherited somewhat diminished estates; but he did not in any event have long in which to enjoy what he had or to turn his energies to rebuilding the family fortunes. For, like one of Mary Livingstone's grandfathers and both of Mary Fleming's, he died at Flodden.

Mary Seton's father was twice married. His second wife, Marie Pieris, was one of the ladies-in-waiting who had accompanied Mary of Guise from France on her marriage. He died in 1550, and his son George, the fifth Lord Seton, played a distinguished part in the queen's affairs. He was one of the commissioners appointed to attend the young queen's marriage to the dauphin in France in 1557, when his pleasure must have been heightened by the prospect of a family reunion. He remained faithful to the Catholic faith, but not blindly so: as a young man he was sufficiently interested in the Reformed church to listen to one of its leading preachers, John Willock, expounding the doctrines of the new religion from his deathbed. His eventual decision to remain within the church of Rome, and with the party of

ABOVE LEFT *The Seton family were amongst Mary's staunchest adherents, and suffered considerably in her cause. This portrait was painted in 1572 by Frans Pourbus.*

ABOVE *The Seton Armorial's representation of Mary and Darnley. They passed their honeymoon at Seton.*

the dowager queen, was looked on with especial disfavour by the Lords of the Congregation, especially as at the critical time of 1559 he held the important office of Provost of Edinburgh.

On Mary's return to Scotland as queen, Seton was appointed grand master of her household. He and his principal residences played a significant part at some of the most crucial moments of Mary's reign: Seton House in particular was a favourite retreat for her, not too far from Edinburgh. Her marriage to Darnley (who was also Seton's cousin) in 1565, 'with not more than seven persons present', was followed by a short honeymoon at Seton; and, by a strange twist of fate, it was there that she also spent the last night of her short married life with Bothwell.

George, the fifth Lord Seton, was to the fore in both of Mary's spectacular escapes. On the night of her flight from Holyrood after Rizzio's murder in March 1566, it was at Seton House that she first drew rein. But Seton itself was too near Edinburgh to be safe, so together with loyal nobles including Lord Seton and the Earls of Bothwell and Huntly, she headed eastwards towards the fastness of Dunbar. Darnley, beside himself with fear, was undeterred by Mary's plea for the safety of the child of her seven months' pregnancy, retorting callously, 'If this one dies we can make another.'

To Seton she came again a year later, her nerves shattered by another murder: that of Darnley. The Setons' efforts to occupy her mind with everyday pleasures went badly awry: scandalous reports reached the capital that the queen, instead of submitting to seemly mourning, was spending her time in such carefree pursuits as hunting and archery.

The splendid Seton House of Queen Mary's day was a relatively recent structure, for the major part of the old castle had, like so many others, been looted and destroyed during Hertford's invasion of 1544. The newer portion, disposed around a triangular courtyard, was added to in the seventeenth century, but the building described by one eighteenth-century traveller would have had a lot of similarities with the one Mary knew and loved so well:

The House consisted of two large fronts of freestone, and in the middle is a triangular court. The front to the south east hath a very noble apartment of a Hall, a Drawing Room, a handsome Parlour, Bedchamber, Dressing room and closet. This apartment seems to have been built in the Reign of Mary Queen of Scots; for on the ceiling of the Great Hall are plastered the Arms of Scotland, with the Arms of France on one hand ... The front to the North seems to be a much older building than this. The apartments of the state are on the second story, and very spacious; three great rooms, at least forty feet high, which they say were finely furnished, ever since Mary Queen of Scots, on her return from France, kept her apartments there.

Of today's Seton House, a modest but attractive structure in comparison with what went before, only the barrel-vaulted ground floor dates from the sixteenth century.

The other Seton house, at Niddry, played an even more dramatic part in the life of Queen Mary. Lord Seton was instrumental in arranging her escape from Lochleven in 1568. It was he who welcomed her ashore to temporary freedom, and it was to Niddry that he conveyed her that night, her hopes high and her courage restored. She was warmly received by the local population: 'Quhen she has come to the land they horsett her immediately with gladness on all sides.'

Before long all their hopes were in shreds, and Seton himself was taken prisoner at Langside. His estates were forfeit and he remained a prisoner until 1569, managing nevertheless to stay in contact with Mary and delivering countless petitions on her behalf to Elizabeth. He was allowed to go into exile in France, where he endured great penury and at one time was reduced to driving a wagon for his livelihood. But when James VI came to

power he reinstated him, and he ended his days as ambassador to France.

His sister was the only one of the Maries not to marry. She remained in the queen's service and shared her English captivity for fifteen years, until, with failing health, she retired to a convent at Rheims in France. At the time of her admission to the convent, where she lived on until her seventies, the abbess was Mary's aunt, Renée de Guise.

The castle which sheltered Mary during that brief taste of freedom was probably begun by the third Lord Seton around 1511. He cannot have had time to see much of the results of his vision, for two years later he lay dead on Flodden field. His widow supervised the work until the fourth earl came of age. He in his turn repaired and extended the building in 1539, and had the castle confirmed as a free barony. As well as financial advantages, this gave him the right to imprison or hang offending tenants, a privilege of which the Lord Seton of Mary's day made full use when he occupied Niddry in 1567.

Niddry continued in the possession of the Seton family until 1676, when it was sold to the Hopes, who occupied it for thirty years while they awaited the completion of their magnificent Hopetoun House, designed by the brothers Adam. Thereafter they deserted Niddry for the seclusion of the grand new house and parklands near the Firth of Forth. By the mid-nineteenth century the Union Canal and the Edinburgh-Glasgow railway line both ran through its grounds, and in the 1860s shale-mining for the extraction of oil began, and industry moved in. The abandoned castle, meanwhile, itself became a useful quarry for materials for later buildings.

Today the castle is a sorry sight, a blackened crumbling ruin, daubed with anglophobic graffiti, and all but swallowed up by a shale bing. It is all the more remarkable therefore to discover that an exciting restoration project is in hand. In 1985 the Hopetoun Estate sold the ruins through the National Trust for Scotland, who are assisting the new owners, two young schoolteachers, Peter and Janet Wright, in a bold effort to bring the castle back to life. Because of their imaginative scheme we can look forward over the next decade to seeing one of Mary Stuart's most dramatic resting places come to life again, a fitting memorial to the Seton family.

Mary Fleming's ancestry was not merely noble but royal, for like the queen she had James IV for a grandfather. There is some confusion about the identity of her grandmother, who is sometimes given as Jane Kennedy, one of his earlier and most regular mistresses, and sometimes as Lady Agnes Stewart; but the evidence points to the latter lady, afterwards Countess of Bothwell.

Lady Janet Fleming had six children by her husband, and a son by the King of France while she was governess to the young Queen Mary. For this indiscretion – and, so the story goes, for her public flaunting of her condition – she was sent home to Scotland, to the Fleming seat at Boghall Castle, Biggar. If the remains of Niddry are still well visible, and the prospect of its restoration a feasible proposition, the same cannot be said of Boghall. Only a few crumbling ruins in a cow pasture stand testament to what was once an important castle at the strategic point where the valleys of Tweed and Clyde all but join.

But the church in Biggar, which dates from the days of Lady Janet and her husband, Lord Malcolm, still stands. It is believed to be the last church to be built in Scotland before the Reformation, and is largely unchanged since those days. A strange feature is the irregularity of its cruciform shape: obviously the walls of the choir, constructed from without and then broken through a temporary wall to join the rest of the building, were not properly aligned. The town of Biggar is worth a visit for this church and much else, and a link with the Fleming family remains in its annual March Riding celebrations. The young girl chosen to preside over the festivities is known as the Fleming Queen, supposedly a reminder of a day

*The ruins of Seton House, much visited by Mary and thought to have been extended for her convenience.*

*Two views of the Seton castle
of Niddry, now under
restoration, where Mary
spent the night after her
escape from Lochleven.*

when Mary Fleming, at her cousin's request, held royal sway for a day.

Lord Malcolm died at Pinkie Cleugh, just as his father had died at Flodden. His eldest son, like Lord Seton, went to Paris for the marriage of the Scots queen and the dauphin; but he did not return. Along with three others he was taken ill and died on the journey home, supposedly the victim of a French poison plot.

Lord Malcolm's second son John, the fourth Lord Fleming, succeeded. He was closely associated with the activities of the court, and a measure of the regard in which he was held is exemplified by the sumptuous wedding feast which the queen arranged for him on Arthur's Seat, overlooking Edinburgh. As we have seen, he continued to hold Dumbarton Castle on her behalf for several years after her English imprisonment.

Mary Fleming herself married the nimble-witted Maitland of Lethington, the queen's secretary and the most subtle Scottish politician of his day. She must have found herself the victim of conflicting personal loyalties when, after Mary's marriage to Bothwell, Maitland deserted their cause and joined the rebelling lords. But eventually he returned to the fold, and was one of those who held Edinburgh Castle for her until 1573, when it fell to the invading English. On capture by them, he evaded the executioner's axe by committing suicide.

There is no portrait, unfortunately, of Mary Fleming, who seems to have inherited a great deal of the Stewart beauty and charisma. Bishop Leslie described her as 'the flower of the flock'; the English agent Randolph called her 'a Venus for beauty, a Minerva for wit, and a

*The ruins of Boghall Castle, once the seat of the Fleming family.*

Juno in wealth', and George Buchanan, during the time when his description of Queen Mary's court consisted of panegyrics rather than defamation, gave her the sobriquet 'Queen Flaminia, to whom virtue has already supplied a sceptre'. Maitland's courtship of this lovely young woman occasioned gossip and even ribaldry among the court circle: he was a widower in his forties and she took some time, it seems, to make up her mind. The marriage did not take place until January 1567, the fateful year that was to see such an upheaval in the fortunes of her mistress. She remained loyal to Maitland even after his death, when she begged successfully that his body should be spared the indignity of a post-mortem treason trial. She outlived him by many years, bringing up her children in somewhat distressed circumstances.

In many ways Mary Beaton's family – not strictly speaking of noble blood – was the most interesting of all the Maries'. Indeed, the Beatons of Fife were one of the most powerful and intriguing clans in the whole of sixteenth-century Scotland. The Beatons (or Betouns, or Bethunes) had come to Fife from Picardy in northern France: the large families they produced seem on the whole to have survived into adulthood, and the different branches of the family are often confused. The most famous of all, Cardinal David Beaton, who reached the peak of his power during the regency of the Earl of Arran, is usually referred to as being an uncle of Mary Beaton, when in fact he was her grandfather's cousin.

Mary's branch of the family was that of the Beatons of Creich, who had a modest estate roughly midway between Cupar and the abbey of Balmerino in Fife. The first Laird of Creich was Lord High Treasurer to James IV, with whom he had reputedly been brought up 'like a brother'. Mary's father and grandfather were both keepers of Falkland Palace and masters of the royal household; her mother, Joanna de Lareyneville or Gryssoner was another of Mary of Guises's ladies-in-waiting, and must have been an especial favourite, for as well as contributing to her dowry, Mary also provided 'cramossy velvet' for Joanna's bridal gown.

Mary Beaton's father, Robert, had many sisters, several of whom were prominent among the women of their time. Elizabeth was a mistress of James V and bore him a child, generally identified as Jean, Countess of Argyll (who, with her uncle Robert, was present at the fateful Holyrood supper party that ended in Rizzio's death). Margaret, Lady Reres, was wetnurse to James VI; and Janet, the eldest sister, though thrice married, in middle life became the lover of the young Earl of Bothwell, and in popular gossip was implicated with him in the explosion and murder of Darnley at Kirk o'Field.

As the middle-aged Maitland courted young Mary Fleming, so Mary Beaton also attracted the attentions of an older man. This was Queen Elizabeth's ambassador, Thomas Randolph, who was sufficiently certain of his success with the lady-in-waiting to make the outrageous suggestion that she should spy on her royal mistress on his behalf. It must have been with some relief that she received the attentions of Alexander Ogilvie of the Boyne, a suitable young Scotsman whom she subsequently married.

If the ruins of Niddry Castle are now dwarfed and ravaged by industrial development, the same cannot be said of the old Beaton home of Creich, although physically it is in much the same state. It lies up the quietest of roads, a stone's throw from the ruined church of the same name, protected by little whin-clad hillocks and with a lochan at its base. The walls are covered in moss, lichen and ivy, and drifts of leafmould are banked against the walls. Set so far away from other settlements, it has not suffered the fate of so many buildings of its time – being used as a convenient quarry for house-building of later centuries. The decorative corbelling work, and the relative thinness of the walls, indicate that Mary Beaton's grandfather built it as a domestic rather than a defensive structure.

OPPOSITE *The parish church of Biggar, built by Mary Fleming's father and thought to be the last pre-Reformation church constructed in Scotland.*

BELOW *Sir William Maitland of Lethington, Queen Mary's able secretary of state and, in time, the husband of Mary Fleming. Though disillusioned with the queen at the time of the Bothwell wedding, he returned to her cause and died in her service.*

Mary Livingstone's father, the fourth lord, was appointed one of Mary Stuart's guardians in 1545 and sailed in her entourage to France three years later. Like the fathers of Mary Beaton and Mary Seton, he also had a French wife. It may well have been this connection that led Mary of Guise to choose the little girls as companions for her daughter; and, conversely, it may have been the mothers' affection for the dowager that led them to name the girls in her honour.

But by the time of their return, the fourth lord was dead, and Mary's brother had inherited the title. Livingstone's loyalty never wavered, but like Bothwell he held religious and political beliefs that were contradictory, for his personal loyalty to the queen was combined with an adherence to Protestantism. But his religious commitment seems to have been of a most pragmatic variety: it did not exclude him from attending the Catholic baptism of Prince James (an event from which Bothwell felt obliged by his conscience to absent himself); he was one of the very few nobles who attended the queen's ill-fated third marriage ceremony; and he went with her into exile in England.

Mary Livingstone was the first of the quartet to marry. Her husband was John Sempill, a son of Lord Sempill, another family of great loyalty to the queen's cause. Knox, with his vicious taste for gossip, claimed that the marriage had been hastened, presumably for the usual reason. But as with so much of Knox's malicious talk, the facts are at variance with the picture he wished to present. Mary Livingstone's well-planned nuptials took place amid great splendour early in 1565, her mistress paying for her gown and the wedding feast and contributing handsomely towards the dowry, and her first child was born a year later.

Mary Livingstone's last service to her mistress seems to have been after the débâcle at Carberry Hill when, taken in disgrace and hysteria back to Edinburgh, the queen was allowed a couple of hours' grace at Holyrood with Mary Seton and Mary Livingstone.

Mary's family home, the old Callendar House at Falkirk, is now completely different from the structure that existed in her day. A convenient stopping place for the queen on visits to and from the west, it is not rich in historical associations like Seton or Niddry, nor does its present appearance (it was until recently part of a modern college of education) conjure up the atmosphere of the past that attaches to the walls of Creich and even to the stones of Boghall.

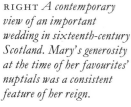

RIGHT *A contemporary view of an important wedding in sixteenth-century Scotland. Mary's generosity at the time of her favourites' nuptials was a consistent feature of her reign.*

OPPOSITE *Another view of Creich, giving an impression of its decorative details. Its relative nearness to Falkland made it easy for the head of the household to be the keeper of the king's palace there.*

# 10

## FRIENDS AND RELATIONS: HOMES AND FAMILIES

*Craigmillar Castle, on the outskirts of Edinburgh, was the home of Sir Simon Preston, provost of the city.*

On Mary's return to Scotland in 1561 as an adult, reigning queen – the first in the annals of Scottish history, though the nation had become used to the machinations of powerful dowagers – she was more isolated than any of her recent predecessors. She had few memories from her early childhood in her native land, she had never seen her future lying there, and all her friendships and family connections were those she had established in France. Her forebear James I, it is true, also spent his youth abroad; but his return to Scotland and his freedom from an English prison were a goal for which he had yearned for years, and, moreover, he came back with the support and love of a strong and able wife. Mary's other deprivations pale into significance beside the loss of her young husband.

So where was she to find friendship, with whom was she to pass the leisure hours? Whose homes were to be graced by her, in place of the rich French châteaux she had left behind? She might expect to find such companionship among three groups of people over and above her special relationship with the Maries. In this chapter we look at an example from each of these groups.

The natural place to look for close friendship was among her numerous step-siblings and cousins, all of them descendants of James IV and James V. Apart from her cousin Mary Fleming, and Lord James Stewart, later Earl of Moray, with whom she had an ambivalent relationship, half brotherly affection and half frustrated and deposed rivalry, there were two with whom she seems to have had an especially close relationship. One was her only sister, Jean, Countess of Argyll, to whom she is said to have been particularly drawn on account of her unhappy marriage to the Earl of Argyll. Mary singled her out for special regard in the will which she drew up as her confinement approached in June 1566.

But she seems to have been fondest of all of her brother, Lord John Stewart, her father's son by Elizabeth Carmichael. He was not much older than herself, and with another brother, Lord Robert, accompanied her to France as a child. He appears to have stayed there for some time and to have made later visits, for he was also among the train that accompanied her return. He was not however among the commissioners who attended the French marriage. Perhaps he lacked the requisite gravitas, in spite of the respectable-sounding title of Commendator of Coldingham, which his father had bestowed on him. As James V had approached marriage, first with Princess Madeleine and then with Mary of Guise, he established security for his previous offspring by arranging for them the benefits of such offices, which should of course have gone into religious and not secular hands. The income derived from Coldingham was indeed valuable.

The religious settlement far down on the Berwickshire coast has a long ecclesiastical history stretching back to the seventh century, when it was part of the kingdom of Northumbria. But it grew in significance when at the end of the eleventh century the little-known Scots King Edgar granted 'Coldingham and all the land they have in Lothian' to the

Benedictine monastery at Durham. When Edgar himself came to the dedication of the church at the turn of the century he made other grants of land. His subjects subsequently imitated him, until the lands of Coldingham stretched from the Scottish burgh of Berwick (at one time holding one-seventh of the entire population of the country) to Auldcambus in the north and Kelso in the east, in addition to scattered holdings as far away as Fife. The church soon expanded into a priory, which was substantial enough to accommodate the Scottish court from time to time. Its slightly anomalous situation as a dependency of Durham rather than of a Scottish monastery seems to have been managed with tact and good sense – but it did not save it from being sacked on a punitive expedition of King John's in 1216.

*The ruins of Coldingham Priory. Mary's favourite brother, Lord John Stewart, was commendator (lay abbot) of the priory.*

What remains of the priory today dates from the reconstruction that then followed. The present parish church was carved out of the thirteenth-century remains in the middle of the last century, and is a much more sensitive restoration than most Victorian architects and builders achieved by imposing the ideas of their own century on the work of previous ones. The north wall, facing the visitor, must surely be one of the loveliest to grace a village parish church anywhere in Scotland, its delicate arcading reaching unspoiled across seven centuries. The uncompromisingly stark reconstructed south wall would be uninspiring on its own, but as a foil to the incomparable medieval vestiges it is wholly appropriate.

Outside, the ruined walls of the domestic part of the priory give only the sketchiest notion of the extent of the foundation to which Lord John Stewart fell heir: most of it has been quarried to build the lovely village that has grown over the centuries at Coldingham. But even in Lord John's time the religious life had all but gone: the greed of the Home and Douglas families, not to mention that of the royal house, meant that the temporal riches of Coldingham had assumed supremacy over its spiritual duties.

The regularization of the priory's international position by its annexation to Dumfermline in 1509 did not help: it merely made its riches more accessible to the crown. From the beginning of the sixteenth century the numbers of monks at Coldingham were in single figures: its splendid occasions were secular ones, such as the reception in her northern bridal progress of James IV's teenage queen Margaret Tudor.

Lord John was not the first half-royal recipient of Coldingham's revenues, though his predecessor was probably more suitable. Alexander Stewart, the beloved and precociously brilliant oldest son of James IV, had combined the commendatorship of Coldingham with the archbishopric of St Andrews. He was at least fitted for the church by inclination, and for high office by intellect, and might have brought great credit to the church in Scotland as the ripples of reforming unrest reached its shores from Europe; but, like so many other promising young men of his generation, he died at Flodden.

Lord John, the Archbishop's nephew, on the other hand, appears to have been high-spirited and totally unsuited to even a nominal church office. What glimpses we have of his short life show us a young man who, along with another brother, Lord Robert Stewart (holder of yet another lucrative church office, that of Commendator of Holyrood), and Mary's young Guise uncle, the Marquis d'Elboeuf, seems to have been the instigator at his sister's court of at best grace and spectacle, and at worst unmalicious mischief. Today's tabloids would have found them good copy.

We discover Lord John, for example, leading one of the two teams of six competing at 'running for the ring' in a tournament in November 1561, a team dressed in women's clothes, moreover, (who defeated d'Elboeuf's 'strangers'). Less respectably, and this time in company not just with the Frenchman but also with Lord Bothwell, he was involved in an incident that was the scandal of the capital – especially of those who wanted an excuse to be shocked by Bothwell. It concerned a merchant's daughter, Alison Craig, who, rumour had it, had engaged the affections and seduced the person of the puritanical Earl of Arran. The antics of the trio were indeed reprehensible: they included first a disguised, and then a forced entry into Alison's house in the hope of finding Arran *in flagrante delicto*. In this ambition they failed, uproar in the city followed, and the church denounced the behaviour of the participants with pious indignation: 'The horror of these facts commoted all godly hearts to crave upright and true judgements against such persons as have done what in them lies to kindle God's wrath against this whole realm. The impiety committed is so heinous and so horrible that we should think ourselves guilty if we pass it over in silence.'

Excuses were found for the queen's relations: d'Elboeuf was a foreigner, Lord John was too young to know better. In truth he can only have been at most a couple of years younger

than Bothwell, on whom the opprobrium for the incident and its aftermath fell. But over a few years the latter had managed to build up a fairly impressive collection of political enemies. His friendship with Lord John, however, was soon to be cemented by the commendator's marriage to Bothwell's sister, Lady Janet Hepburn.

Lord John's wife was herself not without notoriety. Some years earlier she had been engaged to marry the son of an East Lothian laird, an arrangement that would have had financial benefits for her hard-pressed father. On the latter's death, she quickly disentangled herself from the forthcoming marriage, and seems to have used her freedom with a certain indiscretion. In 1560 she was the subject of court gossip which even the scandal-mongering English ambassador Randolph judged too risky to put on paper; and John Knox's typically sour comment on the marriage of the two young people was 'a fitting woman for such a man'. They do indeed seem to have suited each other well during their short time together.

Lord John died on a witch-hunting expedition to Inverness with his brother Lord James in early 1563, the year that witchcraft became a statutory offence in Scotland for the first time. The exact circumstances of his death are not known; but his sister's grief and her continuing care for the widow and for his child Francis are well documented. She continued to make presents to her sister-in-law, and Francis was especially remembered in the will she made three years later. At the news of his father's death, she had cried bitterly and bemoaned the fact that 'God always took from her those she loved best'. She had just lost two of her Guise uncles on whose advice she had always relied, but Lord John's death must have greatly increased her sense of personal isolation in Scotland.

A year after the marriage the queen had been on a very private visit to Coldingham to join their new year celebrations. She returned to Coldingham once more, at the end of her expedition to the Borders in the autumn of 1566. Looking at the ruined foundations today, it is difficult to imagine that the walls which rose from them once accommodated a royal party and, reputedly, a thousand followers. That was Coldingham's last mammoth occasion. In the next century it was besieged and vandalized by Cromwell, but the destruction was not irrevocable: out of the remains, where monks for almost a millennium praised God through their lives and devotions, has been created what must surely be one of the most beautiful small parish churches in Scotland today.

Amongst the Scottish nobility the Erskine family held a position of special closeness to the queen. As we have already seen, one of her guardians as a young child was the fifth Lord Erskine, and Erskines were also appointed guardians to her father and her son.

The family originally took their name from the barony of Erskine in Renfrewshire. An Erskine daughter married into the family of Robert the Bruce; another became the wife of Walter the Steward – though history does not relate whether this was before or after the latter became son-in-law to the great king, and begetter through Margery Bruce of the house of Stewart. In the mid-fourteenth century the family achieved great prominence. Sir Robert de Erskine held the important offices of Lord High Chamberlain, justiciar north of the Forth, and constable of the three major castles of the realm: Edinburgh, Stirling, and Dumbarton. He was ambassador to England and to France, and it was for his services to Robert II that he received the estate of Alloa. Situated on the banks of the Forth, a short ride from Stirling Castle, and surrounded by the then extensive forest of Clackmannan – the hunting and grazing of which were included in the grant – this was a highly desirable acquisition. By the following century the keepership of Stirling Castle was firmly in the hands of the Erskine family, where it remains to this day. Although they were denied their hotly disputed claim to the earldom of Mar, lands and holdings far and wide were granted or confirmed to them by the king. Apart from the traditional baronies of Erskine and Alloa, these ranged as far as Kellie in Aberdeenshire and Nesbit and Dalgliesh in Roxburgh.

*The sixth Lord Erskine, childhood friend of the queen, ennobled as Earl of Mar in 1566 after the birth of Prince James, with whose guardianship he was entrusted.*

It is difficult to give an exact date to the original structure of Alloa Tower. As late as 1489 the original charters give no hint of a building of such magnitude there; but from eight years thereafter the word *castrum* is used to describe it, and the erection of such a building at about this time is also supported by architectural evidence. At the same time the hamlet of Alloa was beginning to expand. It became a river port of some prominence, especially as the forest of Clackmannan, like that of Fife, was hewn down on the orders of James IV to provide materials for the substantial Scottish navy that he was building up. Shipbuilding appears to have taken place at Alloa, and it is at this time that the first mention of coal-mining appears: the industry on which the industrial town was to rise in later centuries.

It was through the Erskines' keepership of Stirling Castle that they came to make their most important contribution to history, as guardians of the infant monarchs of Scotland. In face of the aggression of Henry VIII, first after Flodden and later during the 'rough wooing', Stirling was a safer royal nursery than any other castle. A contemporary, quoted in a recent publication by Clackmannan District Libraries, *A Short History of Alloa*, gives an interesting insight into the duties of the guardian of James V, and it can be assumed that similar arrangements were made in respect of his daughter:

As a tutor, he has to teach his royal pupil in all good virtues and to read and write in Latin and French; and to sleep in his chamber at night. The guard is to be made up of twenty footmen, who take turns of watching all night by fours, and these receive the watchword from none other than Lord Erskine himself. The king is to dine at a table by himself, while Erskine dines at another board in the same room with the captain of the guard and others. If the young king goes outside to the park, it must be in secret and in 'right fair and soft wedder [weather]' while some six or eight horsemen scour the country ahead of him.

Although these precautions did not prevent James from being seized by the Douglases and held by them for many unhappy years, he continued to hold his old guardian in affection and confidence, and in time nominated him as a potential governor of the kingdom. The fifth lord's closeness to the king was also strengthened by his position as an unofficial father-in-law: James's great love Lady Margaret Douglas, mother of Lord James Stewart, was one of his daughters.

Queen Mary's guardian died in 1555, predeceased by his eldest son who had been killed at the battle of Pinkie. It is claimed that his successor, John, was a boyhood friend of the queen, and of course he may well have frequented the nurseries at Stirling or accompanied his father to France in 1548. John seems originally to have been destined for the church, but was thrown into the traditional Erskine occupation of keeper of royal castles by his succession to the title. He was therefore especially close to Mary at that highly vulnerable period of her life, the birth of her son, under his protection, at Edinburgh Castle. Four days after the confinement, the grateful queen granted Erskine the title that his family had sought for well over a century: the earldom of Mar.

It was in the period after the birth of Prince James that Mary visited the Mars at Alloa Tower, apparently in order to recuperate, though one would have thought that the damp air around the low-lying Forth was not the most therapeutic in Scotland. But in this period after the traumas that surrounded the murder of Rizzio and the birth of her child, Mary's exhaustion was of the mind, and the companionship of the trusted noble who had recently been so close to her was no doubt restful. It is interesting that she made the journey by ship; she was followed by the estranged Darnley who came by land, 'to be awkward', according to one source. One tradition has it that a reconciliation was effected at this time; another that the conjugal visit lasted only a few hours.

The building where this recuperation and possible reconciliation took place is still in possession of the Mar family, and in relatively good order (though difficult to find, situated

*A nineteenth-century impression of Craigmillar Castle. Here, during Mary's convalescence in November 1566, the plot to eliminate Darnley was hatched.*

as it is in the heart of the woollen mills that house one of Alloa's main industries). This is despite an extensive fire in 1800 which destroyed the roof and many of the Mar family possessions, including what was reputed to be the only authentic portrait in Scotland of Mary Queen of Scots.

The queen's last visit to the Earl of Mar, guardian of her son, has already been chronicled. In the clash that followed, he threw his weight behind the rebel lords led by his sister's son, the Earl of Moray. But his loyalty was above all to the person with whose care he was entrusted; the young King James VI. Mar's defection indicates the dissatisfaction that was rife amongst the nobles after Mary's marriage to Bothwell. Even amongst those with long records of steady loyalty and royal favour received in return, support melted like snow off a dyke. The pattern was repeated through all levels of Scottish society, including that immediately below the nobility – the lairds.

One of these who had received special favour from the queen was Sir Simon Preston of Craigmillar. Both he and his home were to play a significant part in the events of the times. Craigmillar Castle is a substantial building, right on the southern boundary of modern Edinburgh. The rooms are spacious and numerous, and the Preston lands, which now contain one of the city's largest housing schemes, stretched as far as the royal hunting park surrounding Arthur's Seat. The castle itself is in a stupendous position, second only to that of Edinburgh Castle itself: from it can be seen the course of the River Forth to the west; to the east and south are the valleys of the two Esk rivers; and to the north, across the Forth, are the hills of Fife.

The name derives from the Gaelic 'Craig Moilard', meaning a high rock descending to a plain. Whatever the antiquity of the hillock and its settlement, it does not appear in records until 1212, when the family occupying it bore the same name as the land. It was in 1376 that Craigmillar passed into the possession of the Preston family: from then on they were closely bound up with the affairs of the city. As early as 1434 a Preston of Craigmillar was Provost of Edinburgh, and members of the family also served in various parliaments. The bearer of the name during the reign of James II was William Preston. He must have been of a religious turn of mind (some would say superstitious) for he travelled far and wide to secure, on behalf of his native town, the arm-bone of its patron saint, St Giles. This was presented to the church that bears its owner's name, securing for William Preston great glory in death. An aisle was erected over his burial place, and much sculptured testimony of his piety was commissioned. A further honour was bestowed on his descendants: they were to be hereditary arm-carriers in all future ecclesiastical processions. This office disappeared at the Reformation, along with the arm-bone: Sir Simon Preston must therefore have been the last of his family to undertake the duty.

Like his ancestors, Sir Simon was both Provost of Edinburgh and a Member of Parliament, and he is first recorded as having held these offices in 1540. There is no clue in records of his life to support John Knox's tantalizing reference to him as 'a man of very wicked life and no religion'. He seems to have engaged in trade, for we find James V making purchases of cloth from him, and he was married two or three times. His second marriage, in 1542, was to the redoubtable Janet Beaton, who the following year began divorce proceedings on extremely flimsy grounds, and immediately thereafter married her lover. During their brief marriage the Prestons produced a daughter, Elizabeth, and carried out an unsuccessful defence of Craigmillar against Hertford's troops. The castle was burned down, but in recognition of its owners' actions their lands were extended by a grant from the crown.

We hear of Sir Simon again immediately after the death of Mary's first husband Francis II, when he was among the commissioners appointed by his young widow. Why did she place such trust in him? Had he visited France over the intervening period, or was he one of those whom the dying Mary of Guise recommended to her daughter? It cannot have been a random choice, and as a further indication of the favour in which she held him the queen also nominated him, along with Lord Seton, for the provostship in the same year. In 1565 Sir Simon was again Provost of Edinburgh, this time at the queen's insistence, following the enforced deposition of his predecessor who was now out of favour. A further indication of her goodwill came with her grant to him of the keepership of Dunbar Castle. But in her hour of need Preston failed her. Hearing rumours of the murder of Rizzio and the attempted *coup d'état* at Holyrood, Preston arrived at its gates with a body of citizens, having first sounded the alarm. So far he had behaved admirably: but when the lords in the palace refused the queen leave to address the crowd, as they demanded, Preston and the citizens simply dispersed on Darnley's word that she was safe. Perhaps their easy acceptance of his assurances, so blameworthy with hindsight, was more justified than history allows: why, after all, should they have guessed at her husband's treacherous part in the murder? But compared with Bothwell's audacity, and his emergence as the man of the moment, Sir Simon Preston cuts a sorry figure, and Mary's action in removing Dunbar from the one and granting it to the other is wholly understandable.

By the end of the year the queen was at Preston's castle of Craigmillar on a protracted stay. On the face of it, it seems odd that, not being one of the nobility, he should receive such favour: not merely a private visit from the queen, but an official occupation by the entire court. But apart from being the most convenient castle near to the city capable of accommodating such a train, under its original grant Craigmillar was also endowed with quasi-royal status, for the terms of the grant stated that it was to be available for use as a royal residence when required.

And so Queen Mary and her court came to Craigmillar after the Borders progress on which she had so nearly died. Her recovery would be more assured at Craigmillar than at Holyrood, with all its horrifying memories. The words of the French ambassador, du Croc, give us an insight into her state of mind at the time:

The queen is at Craigmillar, about a league from the city; she is in the hands of the physicians, I do assure you not at all well, and I do believe the principal part of her disease to consist of a deep grief and sorrow. Nor does it seem possible to make her forget the same. Still she repeats these words: 'I could wish to be dead.' You know very well that the injury she received is exceeding great, and her Majesty will not soon forget it.

The unforgivable injury was of course that inflicted by Darnley, and it was at Craigmillar that her closest advisers – Moray, Maitland, Huntly, Bothwell and Argyll – began to broach the subject of how she could extricate herself from her disastrous marriage. Darnley's behaviour was by now imperilling the kingdom. That divorce was discussed is a firmly established fact, as is the queen's reaction to the suggestion: that it should neither offend her honour nor affect the legitimacy of her son. That a bond was signed regarding the removal of Darnley is also undisputed. But the bond has not survived, and several crucial questions remain unproven: who precisely were the signatories to the bond? What were the means referred to therein for the elimination of the Darnley problem? And above all, how detailed was Mary's knowledge of the plot, and was Moray among the signatories?

One legend relating to this episode, almost certainly wildly fanciful but deserving of an airing if only as an example of the kind of fantasy that grows up around Mary Stuart, relates that a subterranean passage led from Craigmillar to Peffermill House, where Bothwell allegedly resided during this period, and that this tunnel was used by him and the queen to pursue an adulterous liaison.

What is certain is that at Craigmillar Mary recovered her health to some extent. She appears to have been impressed by its recuperative qualities, for a couple of months later she proposed to bring Darnley there from Glasgow to speed his convalescence from the illness which at the time was called smallpox, but which from pathological evidence and on Bothwell's testimony is now believed to have been syphilis. (Or, if her complicity in the murder plot is accepted, she attempted to lure him there to his death.) But Darnley proved unwilling to go to Craigmillar, prompted perhaps by intuition, perhaps by well-founded suspicion, or perhaps by some plottings of his own against his wife. Whatever the reason, he made the fateful decision to go instead to Kirk o'Field, on the outskirts of Edinburgh. Whether it is to this circumstance that we owe the survival of the fabric of Craigmillar can only be conjectured.

Sir Simon Preston makes another brief appearance in Mary's story in May 1567, when he apparently acquiesced to her marriage with Bothwell. But again he failed her in her hour of need after the subsequent confrontation between loyal and rebel troops at Carberry Hill, for it was to Preston's town house, known as Black Turnpike, that she was taken in disgrace and dishonour. Black Turnpike has disappeared as surely as Kirk o'Field, its only memorial being a nineteenth-century booklet tracing its site. Craigmillar, however, stands in roofless grandeur above the housing estate that bears its name, mute witness to the scheming that took place within its walls in the winter of 1566.

# 11

# THE BORDERS:
# LIVING DANGEROUSLY

*The stout walls of
Hermitage Castle in
Liddesdale. Mary rode here
in October 1566 to visit the
wounded Bothwell, an
innocent episode that has
fired romantic and lurid
imaginations from George
Buchanan on.*

Of all parts of Scotland the Borders suffered most during Queen Mary's reign. This was nothing new. Over the centuries the people of the Borders had received the full force of onslaughts by invading English armies, and had suffered almost as much from the depradations of the defending Scots. On the southern side of the frontier the English marches were little better off, and by the sixteenth century the area was an international buffer state, subject to special policing by wardens – three for each nation – and to a particular legal system designed to deal with the lawlessness that was a by-product of international strife. From time to time, however, the unrest demanded the personal intervention of the sovereign. None had been more assiduous nor more severe in this than Mary's father, whose punitive expedition in 1529 resulted in the summary deaths of the most noted freebooters and led to a certain degree of pacification.

But nothing in the Borders had ever matched the horrors of the 'rough wooing' of Henry VIII, when soldiers under Lord Wharton's command swept through the countryside robbing, burning and killing. His men were not all English by any means – the wild clans of Liddesdale, the Armstrongs in particular, found it to their advantage to take part in the pillaging – but it was the English generals Sir Ralph Eure and Sir Brian Latoun who were granted possession of the spoiled lands. In order to give some idea of the devastation, it is useful to look at the details of the reports sent to King Henry during the autumn and winter of 1543–4, and to relate these to a map of Teviotdale and Ettrick Forest (overleaf).

9 September. By the Armstrongs at Lord Whartons command: at Ettrick, a town of the Lords of Buccleuch, of his own goods, 30 kine and oxen, 200 sheep, one horse.

15 September. By the Armstrongs: at Helmburn, the young Laird of Cranston's lands, 40 oxen and kine, 6 horses and mares, all the insight [household and furnishings] in six houses there.

16 September. By the Armstrongs: the towns of Kirkhope, with the gates of the tower there burnt, Baillielees and Shaws, 400 cattle, 1,200 sheep, all the horses and insighting within the same towns.

21 September. At Midgehope and Thirlestane, of the Scotts' lands, 200 oxen and kine, 20 horses and mares, 5 prisoners, all the insight in the said town.

21 September. By William Forester, etc: at Eldinhope, a town of the Lord of Buccleuch, 40 oxen and kine, and some insight.

9 October. By the Grahams, etc: the Towns of Deloraine and Bellenden burnt, 7 prisoners brought away, 100 oxen and kine, 1 slain.

31 October. By Edward Story and others at Wharton's command: the town of Selkirk with 8 great stacks of corn, and the grange of Huntly with much cattle, and corn burnt.

[?] November. By John Armstrong with other Scotsmen: the tower of Howpaslet spoiled and the keys of the gate brought to Mr Wharton; 16 kine, all the stuff, 6 prisoners, four hurt to death.

7 November. By Anthony Armstrong, John Foster, etc: the town of Borthwickshiels fired and spoiled; 6 prisoners, 60 oxen and kine, 10 horses and nags, all insight, sundry hurt.

8 November. By Robert Forster and others: the town of Whitehillbraes, burnt, 4 prisoners, 40 oxen and kine, 10 horses and nags, all the insight, and sundry hurt.

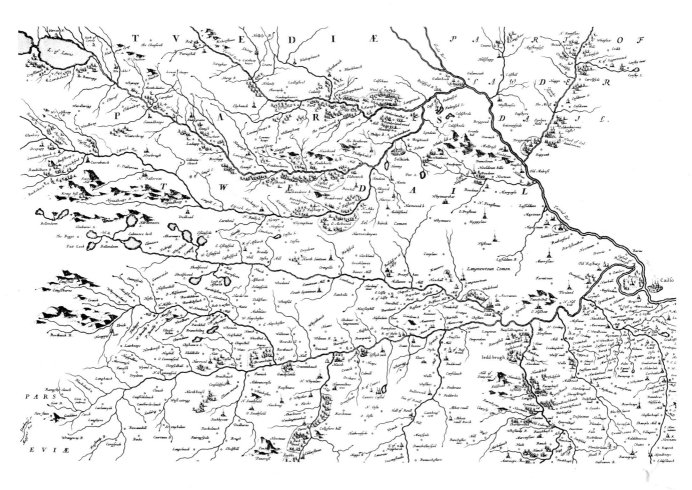

13 November. By Grahams, Fosters, and others: three towns called Essenside, with all the corn in the same, burnt; 1 prisoner, 30 good horses, 60 good cattle.

6 December. By Robin Foster with others: the town of Singlie burnt, 1,400 sheep, 2 prisoners, 2 slain.

*An old map of Ettrick Forest, showing the area that was particularly ravaged by the 'rough wooing'.*

Although it should be remembered that these 'towns' – with the exception of the burgh of Selkirk – are today farms, each of them at that time supported a peel tower and a sizeable community of family and dependants.

The chiefs of some of the Border families, notably the Kerrs, were prepared to co-operate, at the least, with the invading forces, but when a pitched battle was fought at Ancrum Moor in 1545 they rallied to the defence of the queen. The outcome of that encounter was one of the few rays of hope in the weary years of the 'rough wooing': a decisive Scottish victory resulted in the capture of a thousand prisoners and the deaths of eight hundred English soldiers, among them Eure and Latoun. The Scots dead included a girl, Lilliard, whose commemorative stone is the only memorial to the battle:

> Fair Maiden Lilliard lies underneath this stane,
> Little was her fortune, but muckle was her fame.
> Upon the English loons she laid mony thumps,
> And when her legs were cuttit off, she fought upon her stumps.

She is believed to have been one of several women who took part in the fighting.

It was at this time, too, that the great Border abbeys of Jedburgh, Melrose, Kelso and Dryburgh were finally destroyed. The first two in particular had been attacked, burned and rebuilt many times since their foundation in the eleventh century by the saintly King David I. But now they were subjected to the equal pressures of the decaying order within the

*Melrose Abbey, destroyed during the invasion of 1544.*

church and the growing strength of the Reformation, which regarded the beauty of such buildings as inappropriate to the furtherance of worship. Their rich revenues had in any case been appropriated to provide secure futures for powerful local lords or the illegitimate offspring of kings, and the impetus to rebuild was gone for good. They crumbled and were used as quarries until the conservation-conscious twentieth century stopped further decay.

With the arrival of French troops to support Mary of Guise in 1548, the English were gradually driven back from the strongholds they had captured. The French commander, de Beaugué, was appalled at the revenge exacted by the Borderers on their captives: trials of skill at dismemberment were one pastime, while another was to end the life of a shackled prisoner by galloping over his body and stabbing it with a spear (as horses will normally jump over objects on the ground, it is to be supposed that spears and not hooves ended the wretched men's lives). The game of handball still played in Jedburgh and some of the surrounding villages is said to originate from games played with the heads of decapitated English soldiers. The reign of terror was repaid in kind. Constantly in the background, moreover, and a complication in the question of the allegiance of individual clans, were the unforgiving blood feud of the area. Chief of these was the one which raged for nearly forty years between the Scotts and the Kerrs, only to be succeeded by one of almost equal virulence between the Scotts and the Elliots.

Mary of Guise's Lieutenant of the Border in the late 1550s had been the young Earl of Bothwell, who achieved considerable success both in controlling the Scots and in outfacing the English. But he was supplanted in the early years of Mary's personal reign by Moray, who took his duties extremely seriously. In 1563 he arrived in Jedburgh, with full powers to proceed against the thieves of Liddesdale as he saw fit. His zeal far outstripped that of his

*A contemporary woodcut of a hunting scene. The queen is being offered a knife to disembowel the stag.*

father, James v: he burned several peels, hanged twenty-two of the most notorious thieves on the spot, and removed another forty to Edinburgh for trial. Before long he was back, this time at Hawick. Arriving in the town on the day of the winter fair, he found the town full of suspects. Hawick had the reputation of being a great gathering place for criminals, many of whom no doubt disposed of their stolen goods at the fair: according to a nineteenth-century historian 'men who had been publicly outlawed walked abroad, deriding the terrors of justice'. In the hands of Moray, justice was indeed terrible. From the market place he issued a proclamation prohibiting succour to known thieves on pain of death, and to make his point more clearly he peremptorily drowned eighteen of these in a deep pool in the Teviot.

After Moray's fall from favour, Bothwell was reinstated as Lieutenant of the Border. He seems to have had a better understanding of the men who lived there: perhaps their nature mirrored some of his own characteristics, or perhaps the family inheritance of Hermitage

Castle in Liddesdale lent him the necessary authority. When he had escaped from Edinburgh Castle in 1562 he headed for the Borders, and it was noted by Randolph that he could expect to receive help from the 'broken men' there.

Despite Moray's punitive expeditions and the final conciliation of the Scotts and Kerrs, unrest continued. In 1566 it was decided that a royal progress should be made: the queen was to be presented in the Border towns as a figurehead of authority to inspire their allegiance.

The expedition was planned for August, and the Lowland counties were summoned to Peebles on the thirteenth of that month with provisions for fifteen days. But, as so often arises, officialdom had blundered somewhere. August was an impossible month in which to muster an agrarian population: it was harvest time. The royal progress was postponed until October.

It was to have been preceded, however, by an expedition to hunt the game for which Ettrick Forest in particular was so carefully nurtured. Mary decided to fulfil this part of the arrangement. At the time – perhaps because of the approach of their son's important christening – she seems to have been making an effort at conciliation with Darnley, and it may have been to humour his obsession with the thrills of the chase that she went ahead with the hunting. They set off for Meggetland, part of the remote fastness straddling Tweeddale and Ettrick Forest. Here her father had come to hunt, bringing with him from Peebles tented pavilions to house the court. Mary and Darnley stayed at Cramalt Tower, the original site of which, like Meggetdale itself, is drowned under the waters of a modern reservoir. Megget is so remote, and so sparsely inhabited now, that it is difficult to imagine the royal pleasure party there, or the courts that were held by the Stewart monarchs amongst its slopes.

The sport was unsuccessful, and Darnley must have been disappointed. The proclamation issued afterwards in their joint names has about it a similarity to the letter sent not long afterwards by the young king to the Laird of Lochleven:

The King's and Queen's Majesties, understanding that diverse Acts of Parliament and proclamations have been made and set forth prohibiting anyone to shoot at deer with culverins, half-haggs, pistols, or bows, which are plainly disobeyed, and therefore the deer are so wholly destroyed that our sovereigns can get no pastime of hunting, now when their highnesses have purposely repaired in this country to that effect, for remedy of the which in time coming, our sovereigns ordain an officer of arms to pass, and charge all lieges that none take upon hand to shoot deer.

From Megget they went to Traquair, to the house of that name that stands on the banks of the Tweed near the small town of Innerleithen. It had come into use as a hunting lodge for the old Scottish kings, and as long ago as the twelfth century William the Lion had ridden from its tower in pursuit of the game that proliferated in the surrounding forests: deer, wolves and bears. The original tower had been greatly extended by Mary's day, and the house stands very much as she would have seen it. It has welcomed twenty-seven monarchs, and is still occupied by the descendants of her host, Sir John Stewart of Traquair. He was the captain of her guard at Holyrood, and had been one of those who had ridden with her through the night to Dunbar after Rizzio's murder. Perhaps because of that experience he felt a special sense of protectiveness towards her, strengthened by his memories of Darnley's behaviour on that occasion, when he had left the side of his seven-months' pregnant wife to gallop alone into the safety of the night. At any rate Sir John now felt compelled to intervene in an appalling public quarrel between the royal couple under his own roof.

After Rizzio's murder, Mary had vowed never to let Darnley back into her bed again, but as we have seen for some reason she had embarked on a reconciliation of sorts with him. The cause of the quarrel at Traquair shows that in this she had been prepared to go to the limits,

ABOVE *Traquair House,
ancient royal hunting lodge.
It is the oldest inhabited
house in Scotland, still owned
by the descendant of Mary's
host there in the summer of
1566.*

LEFT *Sunlight filters
through the remaining trees
of Ettrick Forest, which
once covered many square
miles and provided rich sport
for the Scottish monarchs.*

Rex et Regina

*This manuscript, preserved at Traquair, bears the signatures of Mary and Darnley. It was while on a visit there that the young couple had one of their bitterest public quarrels.*

for she asked to be excused from the hunting on the grounds that she believed herself to be pregnant again. Darnley's reaction simultaneously confirmed that resumption of marital relations had taken place and probably put an end to them for good: 'What, ought we not to work a mare when she is in foal?' On hearing this Mary broke down before her nobles, and Sir John Stewart was moved to remonstrate with Darnley. Amongst Traquair's many mementoes of royalty, one of the most precious is the cradle Mary Queen of Scots used to rock the infant James VI.

The belated expedition to quell the more unruly parts of the Border set out in October. It was an appropriate time: their summer having been given over to agrarian pursuits, the reivers used the winter months to carry out their raids. Throughout the summer months of 1566, however, the Elliots had been particularly troublesome, promoting their feud with the Scotts and generally creating unrest. As Lieutenant of the Border, Bothwell went ahead of the official party to deal with them. Mary and her train – minus Darnley – made their progress through Peebles and Selkirk to Melrose, where news reached her that Bothwell had been killed in a hand-to-hand encounter with the reiver Jock Elliot of the Park. As further details arrived it became clear that he had in fact survived the attack but lay seriously wounded at Hermitage Castle.

The royal party continued to Jedburgh to hold a justice eyre, or circuit court, the main purpose of the expedition. Mary is reputed locally to have stayed at first at the Spread Eagle Hotel, and the rest of her party discovered that the merchants and innkeepers of Jedburgh, anticipating an influx of wealthy patrons such as had not been seen in living memory, had decided to cash in on the event. Prices escalated and only came down again in response to an edict. The normally litigious Borderers seem to have been overawed by her presence, however, for far fewer cases than were expected came to court. There were grumbles, especially from Moray, about her handling of these – her sentencing policy was regarded as far too lenient. Nobody was hanged or drowned or otherwise disposed of.

Once her business in Jedburgh was completed, Mary set off with Moray and some of the other lords to visit Bothwell at Hermitage Castle, about thirty miles distant. This was the

visit which was to cause so much contention, and to give rise to so many differing interpretations down the centuries. According to Nau, Mary's secretary in later years, who may be presumed to have been speaking for his mistress, 'The Earl of Bothwell was so dangerously wounded that everyone thought he would die. Such being the case, her Majesty was both solicited and advised to pay him a visit at his house, called the Hermitage, in order that she might learn from him the state of affairs in these districts, of which the said Lord was hereditary governor.'

After the events of Kirk o'Field, the Bothwell marriage and Mary's surrender at Carberry Hill, and the 'discovery' of the casket letters, the scholar George Buchanan, who had formerly been one of Mary's supporters, collected the evidence against her in his *Detection*, which gave a different interpretation of these events:

While [Bothwell] was conducting himself there [in Liddesdale] in a manner worthy neither of the place to which he had been raised nor of his family and of what might have been expected of him, he was wounded by a dying robber. He was carried to his castle of Hermitage in a condition such as to make his recovery uncertain. When this news is carried to the queen at Borthwick, although it was a severe winter, she flies like a madwoman with enormous journeys first to Melrose and then to Jedburgh. Although reliable reports about his life had reached that place, her eager mind was unable to retain self-control and to prevent her from displaying her shameless lust. At an unfavourable season, in spite of the danger of the roads and of robbers, she threw herself into the expedition with such an escort as no one slightly more honourable would have dared the entrust with life and fortune.

'Such an escort' included no less illustrious personages than Moray, Huntly and Maitland.

Hermitage Castle, grim, workmanlike, built to defend and to last, stands with its outer walls still intact overlooking the rivulet from which it takes its name. Built in the thirteenth century by the Norman family of de Soulis, it passed into the hands of the Douglases, where, with brief English interregna, it remained for the best part of two centuries. Its history was

ABOVE LEFT *Liddesdale was peopled by unruly clans such as the Armstrongs and Elliots.*

ABOVE *After many years of housing a confused and undistinguished collection of Marian relics, the house where she spent her serious illness in Jedburgh re-opens in the year of the tercentenary of her death as an inspired heritage centre.*

BELOW *This watch, recovered at the spot known as Queen's Mire, is reputed to have been the one lost by Queen Mary.*

particularly savage: an early Lord Soulis had committed such atrocities against his vassals that,

> They wrapped him up in a sheet of lead,
> A sheet of lead for a funeral pall,
> They plunged him into the cauldron red
> And melted him – lead, bones and all.

And a fourteenth-century Douglas owner, infuriated at losing the office of Lieutenant of the Border, starved his successor to death in one of its dungeons.

The castle had been Hepburn property for less than seventy years, but to Bothwell it was the key to his power in the south. When left without sufficient defences it tended to be overrun and occupied by Armstrongs and Elliots, but he had always managed to negotiate or force their departure without much difficulty. But Hermitage was very much a garrison, and no doubt it was the castle's lack of creature comforts which necessitated Mary's round trip from Jedburgh being made in a day. After a couple of hours of businesslike discussion with Bothwell – in Moray's presence – Mary set off to make her way back across Liddesdale. Although it was only mid-October (Buchanan's 'severe winter' must have started early), the evening and the season seem to have been wet. Mary's horse became bogged in a place still called the Queen's Mire, and on her return to Jedburgh the queen fell seriously ill. The ride is commemorated every year during the 'Jethart Callants' festival in July, when a party of riders makes the journey as far as the Queen's Mire. Four hundred years after Mary's journey, the entire ride was reenacted, over the same route and at the same time of year.

Back in Jedburgh, the sick queen was lodged in a bastel (fortified) house belonging to the Kerrs of Ferniehirst. Physically unchanged since then, it still has its garden – in which, inevitably, some of the trees are reputed to have been planted by her – and in the year of the four-hundredth anniversary of her execution reopened as a centre dedicated to her life. In later years she was heard to repeat the sad phrase, 'would that I had died at Jeddart', and indeed she nearly did so. It is difficult now to assess the exact nature and cause of her illness, which has been diagnosed as due variously to nervous collapse, an aggravated ulcer, an attack of haematomasis (an effusion of blood into the stomach), or a disease called porphyria, a hereditary ailment which has hysterical and physical manifestations. According to Maitland, her life was despaired of: she fainted constantly, lost her sight and speech and became so stiff and cold that she was thought to have died. At this point Moray began to make an inventory of her jewels, an action which in many eyes has condemned him more thoroughly than any of his more major acts in opposition to her.

She was seriously ill for over a week, and it was another fortnight before she was able to travel. Darnley visited briefly, but returned quickly to the more important business of hunting, and among diplomatic circles abroad his apparently uncaring attitude was quickly blamed for her illness. In the first week of November she began the journey back to Edinburgh, to her credit fulfilling on the way her original intention of visiting towns throughout the Borders. At Kelso she received a letter from Darnley which, so far from lifting her spirits, led her to declare publicly that death would be preferable to a continuation of her marriage. She paused at Berwick to exchange formalities with the governor, and then took her way through Berwickshire and East Lothian – the heartland of Bothwell's territory.

After Moray had taken over the regency he again visited the fury of his retribution on Teviotdale and Liddesdale, which he harried during the autumn of 1567 with the same enthusiasm as he had shown four years earlier. But the young lairds of the Border, Scott of Buccleuch and Kerr of Ferniehirst, sank their ancient family feud in a concerted effort to support their beleaguered queen, and were among the last to continue to fight for her cause.

# 12

# THE LOTHIANS:
# BOTHWELL'S TERRITORY

*Crichton Castle, the principal seat of the earls of Bothwell, lies about eight miles from Edinburgh.*

James Hepburn, fourth Earl of Bothwell, gallops across the pages of countless novels based on the life of Mary Queen of Scots. *En route* he has picked up one or two biographies of his own, and he is always certain of at least a chapter to himself in any such volume on his wife. It seems difficult for any writer, whether of his own age or a later one, to be objective about him: his personality and his actions allow for no shades of grey. Most commonly he is depicted as the archetypal Border ruffian, the companion of thieves and brigands, emerging from the misty wilds of Liddesdale. He reives and rapes with the best of them, but somehow manages also to be a faithful and reliable servant to Mary of Guise. Later, at her daughter's court, he is perceived as a maverick and an opportunist, a man driven by violent ambition or sexual lust, or possibly both. Then, already guilty of murder and rape, he marries Mary only to desert her for good on the field of battle.

Such, at any rate until this century, has been history's verdict on the third husband of Mary Stuart. It is not surprising that he has had such a bad press – losers nearly always do. But Bothwell has been doubly damned: Mary's enemies include him in their condemnation of her activities, while her apologists find him a convenient scapegoat. Without changing many of the ingredients, the romantic novelists have altered the perspective, linking the downfall of the queen to a sublime passion rather than a seedy affair. Bothwell becomes a Heathcliff-type figure whose approach to every woman is irresistible. But he is still an adventurer. In fact, Bothwell was one of the richest and most powerful nobles of the Scottish court. One must look at the antecedents of his family, at the territory they controlled and the castles they occupied, to understand the man and, as far as is possible, the marriage.

The lands that were once a Hepburn fiefdom cut a swathe through the fertile countryside of East Lothian. It is today the richest agricultural land in Scotland: go there and look at the rich arable fields, at the well-appointed farmhouses and cottages (the more marked because in the 1950s and '60s, when much damage was done to the environment by lax and ugly planning developments, the old county of East Lothian had the luck to be under the supervision of a conservation-conscious planning officer). You can see, too, the modern concomitants of a wealthy farming area: the tidy fences, the sophisticated machinery. No other region in Scotland matches East Lothian for natural wealth, then or now.

Just to the south the lands of Berwickshire – the Merse, the old 'granary of Scotland' – were always subject to cross-border depredations and to endemic rivalry between the factious Border clans. But the lands of East Lothian do not form part of the Borders as such, and though they too suffered – especially during the early years of Mary's reign – they did not do so habitually. The portrait of James Hepburn as a wild Borderer, or any kind of Borderer, is not strictly true. Crichton Castle, near to the source of the River Tyne, is a mere eight miles from Edinburgh: from there the lands fanned out along the river, past the

original Hepburn castle of Hailes. On the coast, the keeperage of Dunbar was traditionally in the Hepburn family.

Crichton, like Hailes, is beautifully set. It is a splendid example of a castle which was originally a simple fourteenth-century keep, and which was later extended around a courtyard. The method of expansion was simple: a length of the surrounding barmkirn (wall) was demolished and a new hall built against the old tower. Not unsurprisingly, there is no record of its building, but we know that by the middle of the fifteenth century it belonged to Sir William Crichton, from whose family it took its name. He was chancellor to James I, who sent him, together with Patrick, the first Lord Hailes – ancestor of James Hepburn – to take possession of Dunbar Castle: it was the latter who became its keeper.

With the exception of a storming and dismantling by a rival family in 1445, history is silent about Crichton Castle until the accession to the throne of James IV in 1488. In the clash that preceded the defeat and death of his father, James had had the support of the eastern lairds Home and Hepburn. Supporting James III against his son had been – *inter alia* – the then incumbent of the earldom of Bothwell, with lands mainly in the area of that name near Glasgow. The latter, along with some allies, was summoned by the new Parliament to stand trial for treason against the new king (a convenient form of retrospective legislation). Like the most famous bearer of his title, Bothwell never stood trial for the charge. By October he was outwith the jurisdiction, but, tried and found guilty *in absentia*, he was sentenced to lose life, lands and goods. He was not heard of again, and it is assumed he found refuge in England. A week later the earldom, including the castles of Bothwell and Crichton, was bestowed on the king's adherent, Patrick, Lord Hailes.

The castle of Bothwell was not strategically important to the new earl, and was on the opposite side of the country from his sphere of influence. The opportunity to exchange it for the more desirable castle of Hermitage came four years later, when James found it convenient to remove the latter from the power-hungry Douglas family and bestow it on his trusted adviser. This then was the extent of the Bothwell lands at their peak: the militarily important castles of Hermitage on the Border and Dunbar on the coast, the rolling lands of East Lothian and two substantial and beautiful castles. With them went various important offices: Master of the King's Household, Lord High Admiral, Sheriff Principal of Edinburgh, Warden of the West and Middle Marches, and Lord of Orkney and Shetland. By virtue of his prominence Bothwell also stood proxy for the bridegroom at the marriage of James to Margaret Tudor.

But the inheritance of the fourth earl in 1556 was sadly depleted. His father – that Patrick, Earl of Bothwell whom we have already seen in pursuit of Mary of Guise – had been made fatherless at Flodden. Psychologists might deduce this to be the source of his lifelong instability; or they could point to his somewhat unjust incarceration at the age of seventeen by James V for showing too little severity to the thieves of Liddesdale. James, of a similar age, was exercising power for the first time and was especially determined to subdue the Borders.

But whatever the cause, Patrick Hepburn's adult life was spent in a series of maladroit attempts to betray either the government of his own country or that of Henry VIII, on whose payroll he so frequently figured. Though the fact that his infidelity extended to include his wife is equally unpalatable, his unsuccessful courtship of Mary of Guise was not wholly unrealistic, nor untypical of the age. The widowed Margaret Tudor, after all, had remarried a Scots nobleman, and then divorced him and taken as her third husband a very minor member of the aristocracy.

His behaviour was remarkable for its inconsistency. Though in English pay, at a time when that country clearly favoured the rise of Protestantism in Scotland he betrayed the gentle Protestant martyr George Wishart. In and out of imprisonment and exile, he was hardly a suitable trustee of his inheritance: his lands were confiscated and he himself was exiled after the Scottish defeat at Pinkie, when the advance of the English troops to Haddington made him a dangerous liability. He returned to Scotland, when Mary of Guise must have been aware that he was a spent force and that his health was failing, for he did not survive long.

James Hepburn, only twenty-one at the time of his accession to the once-powerful Bothwell estate, seems to have been motivated by the desire to restore the family honour and fortune. Yet he too was inconsistent: though a Protestant, he did not adhere to the political movement that accompanied the Reformed religion. Perhaps because his years in France as a student had made him a francophile, perhaps because he felt the need to wipe the slate clean of his father's behaviour towards the queen mother, he was one of a dwindling band of nobles who remained constant to her until her death. She rewarded him suitably, and by the time she died he had recovered the keepership of Liddesdale and the lieutenancy of the Border. But his service to her had engendered the two enmities that were to be his downfall: with Lord James Stewart, the young queen's half-brother, and with the Earl of Arran, next but one in line to the throne.

One episode in particular gave rise to this coolness. In 1559, John Cockburn of Ormiston, another East Lothian laird, was speeding northwards as a go-between of Queen Elizabeth and the confederate lords (including Arran and Stewart) when, the contemporary records state, 'On the last day of October Bothwell with twenty-four men met Ormiston with seven near Haddington, took 6,000 crowns he was bringing to the governor, and hurt him in the face with a sword, whereof he lies at Ormiston.' It was Crichton that bore the brunt of the lords' displeasure:

The governor hearing, sent his eldest son, Mr Maxwell, and the prior, with 700 men to Crichton Castle, Bothwell's chief house eight miles from Edinburgh, put fifty gunners into it on Alhallen day, and lay there that night, returning to Edinburgh the morrow.

On 3rd November, the governor sent his son and Master Maxwell with 300 horse to Crichton Castle, whence they sent to Bothwell at Borthwick Castle to join the Lords: which, he refusing, they spoiled Crichton and brought the spoil and his evidence [title deeds] to the governor.

Bothwell made his escape, but the rift between himself on the one side and Arran and Lord James on the other was deep and permanent, with elements of both a personal and a

political distrust. In time Arran lost his reason, but not before he had seriously damaged Bothwell's standing with Mary Stuart, whose knowledge of Bothwell's loyalty to her mother was already undermined by the persuasions of Lord James, on whom she was at the time almost completely dependent.

When Mary of Guise died Bothwell was on a commission to France, via Denmark, on her behalf. The government was in the hands of his opponents, and his prospects must have looked dim. It was nine months before he returned to Scotland, saddled with a Danish mistress, Anna Throndsen. By this time the young queen had lost her husband as well as her mother, the one person in her life who loved her simply and without thought for her political usefulness. With her widowhood, her position in France tumbled like a house of cards. Her return to Scotland in August 1561 was in a fleet, under the command of the Lord High Admiral of Scotland: Lord Bothwell.

For the first months of Mary's personal reign trouble simmered between Bothwell and his old adversaries of All Hallows' Eve, but thus far it was containable. And the old links between the Hepburns and the royal house of Stewart were now forming again. In 1562 Crichton saw the happiest occasion in its history: the festivities surrounding the marriage of Bothwell's sister, Janet Hepburn, to Lord John Stewart, Commendator of Coldingham, one of the queen's many half-siblings. The romances between the two houses were numerous: the bride's father had been following family tradition in his pursuit of the bridegroom's stepmother nearly twenty years before at St Andrews. Patrick's own mother had been a mistress of James IV, and by him was grandmother to Mary Fleming; and the first and second lords of Hailes were reputed to have been lovers of the widowed queens of James I and James II respectively. But this was the first time that matrimony, albeit between a daughter and an illegitimate son, had been achieved between the two houses.

The marriage was a splendid affair attended by Queen Mary and the court: even Lord James was pressurized by his sister into a temporary suspension of his animosity towards the host. According to Randolph, who was one of the guests, it was an occasion of gastronomic magnificence: 'There were of wild does and roes eighteen hundred, and as for partridges, rabbit, plovers, moorfowl, wild geese, wild duck and drake and other kind of delicate wild beasts – they could not be counted.' After consuming all this the company managed to take part in 'dancing and pastimes and games': the sumptuousness of the whole occasion led the Marquis d'Elboeuf to declare that he had never known such a bridal in France.

This happy affair appears to have been Queen Mary's only visit to Crichton. Not long afterwards Arran's instability and spite led him to make unverifiable accusations that Bothwell and he had plotted to kidnap the queen: on the advice of Lord James, the earl was imprisoned without trial in Edinburgh Castle. After escaping from there he spent two years in exile before being summoned back, in favour once more, at the time of the Darnley marriage and the insurrection of Lord James (by now the Earl of Moray).

Not long after, Bothwell was himself married to Lady Jean Gordon. Under the terms of the marriage contract, he made over to her the life-rent of Crichton, and on their divorce just over a year later, she retained it. Their short married life together seems mainly to have been spent there: certainly it had all the advantages of proximity to the capital and access east and south to Bothwell's other territories.

Nowadays it is a graceful crumbling ruin, magnificent in decay. Its walls still rise to over fifty feet, and the different periods of its building can readily be identified. The original tower stands in the centre of the east side, and the two fifteenth-century wings form the west and south sides of the courtyard. Bothwell had his apartments in the latter part, and this was the castle range as it was in his day. The northern range belongs to the time of Francis, fifth and last earl, nephew of both James Hepburn and Mary Stuart. His are the striking Italianate

*Borthwick Castle, a stone's throw from Crichton. Bothwell found refuge there in 1559 and again, as Mary's husband, when the royal couple prepared to confront the rebel lords. The twentieth century finds it in excellent and unspoiled condition.*

arcades, and the ornamental stonework inspired by the streets of Siena. Even notwithstanding this individualistic architecture, the huge halls and generously proportioned rooms show Crichton Castle to have been the principal residence not of an adventuring upstart but of a noble as powerful as any in Scotland. The last word on Crichton must be left to Sir Walter Scott:

> The Castle rises on the steep
>   Of the green vale of Tyne,
> And far beneath, where slow they creep
> From pool to eddy dark and deep,
> Where alders moist and willows weep,
>   You hear her streams repine.
>
> Not wholly yet hath time defaced
>   Thy lordly gallery fair;
> Not yet the stony cord unbraced
> Whose twisted knots with roses laced
>   Adorn thy ruined stair . . .
>
> Still rises unimpaired below
> The courtyard's graceful portico,
> Though there but houseless cattle go
>   To shield them from the storm.

Eastwards along the course of the Tyne, just a mile or so from the village of East Linton, lie the remains of the original Hepburn Castle of Hailes. It is even more beautifully situated than Crichton, and today's approach to it across a slatted footbridge over the Tyne, which oozes its way between abundant marsh undergrowth, emphasizes its tranquillity. It is a less than strategic situation, and the castle's architects seem to have built for pleasure and not for fortification, unlike the prehistoric inhabitants of the area who chose to build their fortress at the summit of Traprain Law.

Traprain Law erupts strangely into the rolling plains of East Lothian: a landmark for all to see and from which no movement for miles around could be missed. But Hailes faces the slopes of Traprain Law, and its back is protected by the slow-moving Tyne, so in reality its air of defencelessness is illusory. And the sturdy towers, dating from the thirteenth century, together with the subterreanean dungeon pit, speak of the defensive nature of its origins.

There was extensive rebuilding at Hailes in the fifteenth century and further alterations during the next, presumably in the time of Earl Patrick, whose favourite residence it appears to have been. This was the scene of his reception and betrayal of George Wishart, and later he delivered the castle itself into the hands of the English. In February 1548, while an English army under Lord Grey of Wilton was harrying East Lothian, Hailes fell like a ripe plum into the hands of the invaders. Lord Grey was by no means insensitive to the castle's qualities. In his despatches he described it thus: 'The house is for bigness, of such excellent beauty within, as I have seldom seen any in England except the King's majesty's; and of very good strength.'

Hailes is sometimes said to have been a first resting place for Mary on the arduous flight from Holyrood after Rizzio's murder, which eventually took her to Dunbar. She spent a night under its roof when as Bothwell's wife she evaded the army of the rebel lords blockading her at Borthwick. In darkness, wearing men's clothing, she slipped through the night along the Tyne. At Hailes she rejoined her husband, and from there they went to Seton, to Carberry Hill and to surrender.

*Hailes Castle, the original castle of the Hepburn family, lying further east along the Tyne from Crichton.*

If the ruins of Hailes and Crichton are fertile ground for those who seek to conjure up images of the sixteenth century, Dunbar Castle gives nothing away. The very cliffs which were the base of this important and virtually impregnable fort have yielded to the ceaseless onslaught of the North Sea, and its once stout walls have either tumbled into the waves or have been quarried to build the seaside town. It is home today to hundreds of seagulls. Such ruins as there are date only from the time of James IV, but a castle guarded the east coast at Dunbar long before. Edward I joined battle for its possession in 1296, but it was almost forty years later that its most famous siege took place. Blockaded by two great galleys and numerous smaller ships, it was held by the Countess of Dunbar for five months against an English force under the Earl of Salisbury. Lady Dunbar, known as 'Black Agnes', was a woman of great bravery and resource. She took command of the defending troops, and the besieging army is reputed to have coined the following jingle:

> Came I early, came I late,
> I found Black Agnes at the gate.

One of the more fanciful but appealing stories of the siege tells of Agnes and the other women of the castle going out with their handkerchiefs after the bombardments to dust those parts of the battlements which had been hit during Salisbury's attacks. A century later Dunbar was besieged again, and once more a woman played a central part. Queen Joan, widow of James I, defended the castle with the first Lord Hailes, a proximity which supposedly led to the first romance between the Hepburns and the royal line.

For the Scots so strategic a castle as Dunbar was a double-edged sword. In the fifteenth century it fell into English or rebel hands so frequently that in 1488 Parliament ordained it to be 'cassyne doune and alutterly distroyit in sic wise that only fundment tharof be occasion of biging nor reparacione of the said castell in tyme to cum'. But only eight years later none other than the king himself was supervising the rebuilding. As it was a royal structure, we have details of the men who were engaged to built it, amongst them Sir Andrew Wood, the mason Walter Merlione, workman Thomas Berker, and a Dutchman called Hans who gave his name to one of the towers. The measurements of the King's chamber were taken from his corresponding one at Edinburgh, and the buildings were not finished until 1501.

Sixty years later, it had fallen into some dilapidation, but was refortified by the French, who declared that it could now hold five hundred men *more* than before. It must have been gigantic at that time; but the new French extensions were destroyed in accordance with the Treaty of Leith, which ended the long Franco-Scottish alliance in 1560. The demolition was delegated to the lords and barons of East Lothian and their dependants.

When Queen Mary arrived at Dunbar in March 1566, in the company of her most trustworthy lords, she should have been in a state of shock. She had witnessed the barbaric murder of her favourite servant; she had been subjected to manhandling and threats by her nobles; and her escape had necessitated a twenty-five mile gallop from Edinburgh. She had also, in her seventh month of pregnancy, come face to face with the monstrous proportions of her husband's treachery and personal ambition, which did not stop at her safety. The escape to Dunbar shows her at her magnificent best, in small matters as well as large. According to a more reliable legend than that of Black Agnes's handkerchiefs, on arrival at Dunbar she set about cooking eggs for the escape party's breakfast. She must have felt that she was at the nadir of her fortunes, yet she did not collapse. This was one of the finest episodes in the whole of her personal rule. In conference with Bothwell and Huntly she planned moves to defeat the rebels. The loyal lords of the Border were summoned with their men, and orders went out to the rest of Scotland. Thousands flocked to her cause; and on 18 March she rode in triumph back to Edinburgh.

*The ruins of Dunbar Castle, where Bothwell took Mary for safety after Rizzio's murder, and to which he abducted her the following year.*

It was a turning point which carried in it the seeds of ultimate disaster. Bothwell's exemplary loyalty, his bold initiative, his clever organization and command, elevated him in the queen's eyes above her other nobles. Ultimately, in captivity Mary had no alternative but to rely on her own resources, but during her reign she always leaned on the nearest strong man. Her uncles, her brother, her husband had all failed her, but still she needed a male support figure: not surprisingly at this point she turned to the trustworthy Bothwell.

Dunbar was at that time in the keeping of the Laird of Craigmillar, Sir Simon Preston. She transferred it to Bothwell, no doubt as a mark of gratitude to the new recipient, and of corresponding displeasure at Preston's failure to come to her aid. Just over a year later, on 24 April 1567, Bothwell brought her again to Dunbar in the aftermath of another murder. Gallant and resourceful before, she was now in a state of breakdown, worn down by persistent ill-health, exacerbated no doubt by the horrors of the past year as well as by the after-effects of a difficult childbirth. The Kirk o'Field explosion was the last straw.

Whether or not she was actually involved in Darnley's murder, it triggered in her a complete nervous and physical collapse. Placards in Edinburgh's High Street and rumours among the crowds linked her name with Bothwell's, and his with Darnley's murder. And he, despite being accused of having caused the Kirk o'Field explosion and despite being already married (indeed he used his wife as an alibi), pressed the case for his marriage with the queen both on her lords and on Mary herself. Was he acting out of naked ambition, or out of fear of the consequences of Darnley's murder? Was it because he genuinely, though misguidedly, believed that in her state of health marriage to him was the only hope for her continued rule? Or was it (though it stretches credulity to the limits) because their passion for each other was such that they could not live without each other?

There are no neat answers. In April 1567 Bothwell, with a small but effective force,

*After Darnley's murder his father, the Earl of Lennox, led the movement to prosecute Bothwell. But when the latter eventually appeared in court, his armed support was so great that Lennox failed to make a personal appearance and the case was deserted. This memorial painting was done by L. de Vogeleer in 1568 for Lennox and his wife.*

intercepted the queen on the outskirts of Edinburgh as she was returning from a visit to the infant Prince James at Stirling Castle. Mary submitted meekly to him and was abducted by him to Dunbar. Ten days later she rode back to Edinburgh, her horse led by Bothwell. His divorce was under way and she had agreed to become his second – lawful – wife. Whatever happened at Dunbar can only be guessed at: ravishment of the queen; seduction; the administration of drugs or the employment of witchcraft; the simple extraction of a promise to marry from an exhausted and trapped woman; or the culmination of an outrageous plot by adulterous and homicidal lovers: the choice can only be subjective. Only two people knew, and the truth died with them.

Just three weeks later, on 15 May, Mary and Bothwell were married at Holyrood. Within a month after that, outraged by Bothwell's blatant pursuit of power and Mary's possible complicity with him, Bothwell's old enemies among the lords – Moray, Mar, Kirkcaldy, Atholl and others – rose against him and the queen. Moray, conveniently, was in France. They fled from Holyrood to Borthwick, and thence to East Lothian. Betrayed into believing they could in safety return to Edinburgh they set out, and two days later, on 15 June 1567, confronted the rebel troops at Carberry Hill, about eight miles from Edinburgh. Overwhelmed by superior numbers, Mary was persuaded to give herself up to the confederate lords, while Bothwell retreated to the fastness of Dunbar and tried to rally support for her as he had done after Rizzio's murder. But now even clans as loyal as the Scotts found it beyond them to muster to such a tarnished cause and Bothwell, outlawed, was forced north to Spynie and thence to the Orkneys and across the sea to Norway. There Anna Throndsen exacted her revenge on her unfaithful lover, and the remaining decade of the life of that 'glorious, rash and hazardous young man' was spent in Danish prisons.

After Mary's imprisonment in Lochleven and her abdication in favour of her thirteen-month-old son in July 1567, Parliament again ordered the demolition of Dunbar. With the permanent cessation of hostilities with England there was never the need to raise its walls again. The enigma of Mary and Bothwell's stay there was the last chapter in its history.

ABOVE *The memorial to Carberry Hill, where Mary surrendered to the rebel lords without bloodshed, and where she and Bothwell – in a scene of some passion – parted for the last time.*

RIGHT *A contemporary representation of the battle of Carberry Hill.*

# 13

## *LOCHLEVEN: FAMILIAR PRISON*

*Lochleven Castle, Mary's prison for nearly a year, was used by her as a residence in earlier visits to Kinross.*

We regard Lochleven Castle as a sombre comfortless keep, menacingly surrounded by that most impregnable of defences, water: a mean prison house for a queen. Since Mary lived consecutively in Lochleven for longer than any other building in Scotland, apart from her childhood home of Stirling Castle, and since it has such powerful and dramatic associations, it merits a chapter on its own.

Historically, Lochleven Castle was the baronial residence of the feudal superior of the second smallest of the old Scottish counties, Kinross. For 350 years from the late fourteenth century this meant that it was in the possession of the Douglas family. How this came to be, and why it was specially suitable when the time came to hustle the captive queen off to a secure place makes a fascinating tale, as does the wider history of the castle, the island and the county.

Kinross was always one of the more populated parts of Scotland. Its inhabitants are believed to have made a stand against the invading forces of the Emperor Agricola, and were amongst the first recipients of Christianity. The priory of St Serf, once an establishment on Lochleven's second island, claims to be second only to St Columba's Iona in antiquity and was endowed by many Scottish kings over the centuries, including Macbeth. Its tranquil and isolated position seems to have made it a powerhouse of prayer and learning. Amongst its priors were St Ronan, who died in 930, and the early fifteenth-century chronicler Andrew Winton.

According to tradition the castle on the neighbouring island was built at the same time, during the reign of the Pictish King Congal (511–35). None of today's ruins reach that far back into history: the earliest is the square keep, once the only building and well nigh impregnable, which dates from the eleventh or twelfth century. The round tower and the extensive other buildings were probably erected in the early sixteenth century by Sir Robert Douglas around the time of his marriage to Margaret, daughter of Lord Erskine. A carved lintel discovered about a hundred years ago bears the inscription R.D.M.E., their combined initials.

From early times, the castle had an important status both as a royal residence and as a national stronghold. Its pre-eminence can be seen from the instructions to a commission of 1368, during the reign of David II. At a Parliament in Scone held in June of that year, an extensive review of national defences was ordered to be carried out, starting with an inspection of the four royal palaces: Lochleven, Stirling, Dumbarton and Edinburgh.

The castle has already played a part in the affairs of the nation. In 1256 King Alexander III and his wife were seized by members of the Comyn family and carried off to Stirling. The action of the Comyns at this time was regarded as being in the national interest rather than in pursuit of family ambition, for Alexander's queen was the daughter of the English king, and the royal couple were in their impressionable mid-teens. It was felt, and not just by the Comyns, that it would be a wise precaution to keep them under sound Scottish influence.

During the Wars of Independence Lochleven was the scene of one of the exploits of the great patriot William Wallace, as related in the following century by the Scottish poet-historian, Blind Harry. At this time, the castle was garrisoned by the invading force, and Wallace, realizing the 'great skaith', or harm, such a fortress could do to Scotland, planned to capture it. He swam across to the island in his shirt, with his sword tied to his neck, and returned with the garrison's boat. In this he and his men reached the island and stormed the castle, killing thirty of the unsuspecting soldiers. Wallace's panegyrist claims that the hero spared the five women there, since 'woman nor bairn he never caused put to death'.

Twenty-five years later, with her indepedence guaranteed, Scotland was in the grip of a civil war, eagerly abetted by Edward III. At one time, Lochleven was one of only four castles held on behalf of David II against the English king's puppet, Edward Balliol. It was subjected to a siege of more than nine months, under bombardment from boats and from a temporary fort on the lochside erected by the attacking troops under the renegade Sir John Stryvelyne, and suffered a blockade. New English artillery fired stone shot nine inches in diameter. But in November the besiegers took themselves to Dunfermline for a religious festival, and the defenders made a sortie and raided Stryvelyne's fort. Winton, writing a century later on the neighbouring island, claims they took:

> . . . all riches
> that to their liking pleasant was:
> Cross bows, and bows of yew,
> And all thing that might be of service
> Or help them in the pursuit of war.

In that siege, later abandoned, one of the defenders was Sir John Douglas of Dalkeith, the first member of the family to be connected with the castle.

Later in the fourteenth century came the first recorded use of Lochleven as a prison for political offenders, amongst them the future King Robert II and his son. But his captivity there does not seem to have left him with particularly unpleasant memories, for when he ascended the throne he presented the castle to his second wife, Euphemia Ross. Eighteen years later it was a marriage gift to his niece's bridegroom, Sir Henry Douglas, son of the Sir John Douglas of Dalkeith. It was later made over in perpetuity to the Douglases, who in turn increased their power on the separation of Kinross from Fife in 1426. The new shire was placed under the heritable jurisdiction of 'the Lairds of Lochleven', who were granted various rights and privileges, including that of the use of the 'pit and gallows'. The excavation about a hundred and fifty years ago of large numbers of skeletons at the old 'Gallows Hill' seems to prove that the lairds of Lochleven had taken full advantage of this right.

But the crown retained rights in Lochleven even after it had passed into the ownership of the Douglases, much as was done at Craigmillar. It could still be commandeered for state purposes, as happened during the years of Queen Mary's personal reign and earlier, when in 1478 the first Archbishop of St Andrews suffered imprisonment and death there. It was no doubt because of this clause that the Douglases also maintained another 'manour' on the nearest point of the shoreline of the loch.

It is commonly assumed that on her imprisonment at Lochleven Mary was thrust into an unfamiliar keep, but this is far from the truth. She seems to have stayed there frequently, taking advantage of her reserved right of occupation to use Lochleven as a base for hawking excursions in Kinross. As early as 1561 we find her brother Moray ordering four dozen pewter plates, four dozen white iron plates and four curtains of yellow taffeta to be delivered to Lochleven in anticipation of his sister's residence there.

*A portrait of Mary painted by an unknown artist in about 1560.*

The châtelaine of Lochleven was Moray's mother, Lady Margaret Douglas. She had been widowed at Pinkie Cleugh, and left with ten legitimate children to bring up, the eldest of whom, Sir William, was close in age to Moray, her child by James V. It is difficult to pinpoint whether the latter was born before or after her marriage to Sir Robert, and there is no doubt that James tried to secure a divorce for her so that they could marry. For a union of convenience which lasted only about thirteen years, her marriage to Robert Douglas was remarkably prolific.

Lady Margaret is portrayed as a dour, stern woman, disappointed not to have been queen. The irregularity of her relationship with the king must have caused her great anguish later in life when their son's qualities of kingship became apparent. But she must have been rather a strange woman, at the least. A letter written to Moray's wife on the death of a daughter – who apparently lived with her grandmother – is sometimes cited as evidence of her essentially tender heart, but it could equally easily be construed as exhibiting considerable lack of sensitivity in the face of a young mother's grief:

. . . after most hearty commendations, this is to advise your ladyship that it has pleased God to take your daughter, my bairn, to Himself, which is the greatest grief that ever came to my heart . . . none the less I must give thanks to God as I have done in greater matters . . . I pray your ladyship to be of good comfort and treat yourself well that you may live to bring up the lief to be honest folks, for nobody has gotten the greatest loss but I. I doubt not but God shall send your ladyship bairns after this, to do you pleasure, for you are young enough, but there is none able to do me such pleasure as she did . . .

When Lady Margaret's home was requisitioned by the queen early in her reign it was furnished for her in style. A royal presence chamber was established, and the castle was made fit for state occasions. It is thought likely that some of the sixteenth-century buildings around the original tower were also constructed during this period for Mary's benefit. We have details of how Lochleven was prepared for its royal visitor's occupation. The walls of the presence chamber and the bedroom were decorated with ten pieces of tapestry depicting hunting and hawking scenes; the bed was hung with green velvet fringed with silk and made in the form of a chapel, and her counterpane was of green taffeta. Her table-cloth was of green velvet lined with taffeta of the same colour. In the presence chamber the throne's canopy was covered with crimson silk figured with gold, and the draperies were fringed with gold and silver. Other furniture included a small sofa of ebony.

Mary's longest recorded stay before her imprisonment was for a week in April 1563, and it was not without incident. She was visited by John Knox, expostulating against the lack of severity with which anti-Catholic statutes were being pursued. This diatribe, to which she made a moderate and reasoned reply, lasted for two hours. It is not recorded whether or not Knox was invited to stay for the ensuing supper, but the next day the queen requested another meeting with the evangelist. Was it to disarm him that she trustingly asked for his conciliation in the matrimonial problems of her Protestant sister, Jean, Countess of Argyll?

On Mary's marriage to Darnley two years after this, her disapproving half-brother Moray and brother-in-law Argyll planned to kidnap her and remove her to the safety of Lochleven. But just as we are told that the law of precedent is formed in part by the state of a judge's stomach, so in the same way the course of history may be turned by the condition of a man's bowels. At this crucial juncture, Moray himself was confined to Lochleven for four days with violent diarrhoea, and the conspirators' plans were thwarted.

Mary's next visit to the castle was after her victorious campaign against that abortive rebellion known as the Chaseabout Raid. Riding with Darnley at the head of her army, she demanded the surrender of strongholds held by the rebels. Having secured possession of

*Two representations, one nineteenth-century (below, by Samuel Sidley) and one contemporary, of confrontations between Mary and John Knox such as took place on one of her visits to Lochleven.*

Castle Campbell at Dollar from Argyll, she continued her progress to claim Lochleven from Lady Margaret and Sir William, who by now held the castle. They prevailed upon her better nature: Sir William was recovering from an illness, and his young sister-in-law had just given birth to a child in the castle. Mary settled for dinner there – and, presumably, guarantees of good behaviour.

That seems to have been her last free visit to Lochleven and Kinross. Darnley, however, found it a useful bolt-hole during periods of disaffection. In autumn 1566, when his wife lay near to death at Jedburgh, Darnley was busying himself with the problems of sporting facilities in Kinross. From nearby Burleigh Castle he wrote thus to Sir William:

Laird of Loch Leven: Whereas we have taken order through our realm for restraint of shooting with guns, you being Sheriff of those parts we will and command you hereby to apprehend all persons within your charge that so uses to shoot contrary to our order, and we having already understanding of one John Shawe, sun to Maister William Shawe, to be a common shooter, we also charge you hereby to take the said John and send him to us with his gun wherever we chance to be within three days after this present. And further we being informed of divers fires used to be made upon the waters for fishing scareth the fowles, our pleasure is also that ye restrain all such fires being made until ye farther understand from us. In all which doing these signed with our hands shall be your sufficient warrant against all persons. HENRY R.

If the hawking in which Darnley and Mary participated with such enthusiasm no longer takes place, the fishing that so annoyed the young king has survived the centuries. Lochleven yields a rich harvest of a species of trout peculiar to its waters.

The circumstances in which Mary reached Lochleven again were in stark contrast to her triumphant ride at the head of her troops after the Chaseabout Raid. After the débâcle at Carberry Hill on June 1567, when she entrusted herself to the rebel lords, she was taken in captivity through the heering crowds in the Edinburgh streets, and lodged for one night in the town house of her erstwhile adherent, Sir Simon Preston. Her degradation was bottomless. A brief reunion the next day with two of her Maries at Holyrood was interrupted during supper with the command that she make ready to ride with the bullying Lords Lindsay and Ruthven and only two attendants to an unknown destination. She thought initially that they were taking her to Stirling, where she would be with her son and in the company of Lord Mar. The latter might be sympathetic towards the rebels meantime, but there was an old trust and friendship to fall back on. And she knew Stirling well: within its vast staff there would be familiar and trusted faces.

At Lochleven, on the other hand, there was only a tightly knit family, headed by the redoubtable dowager Lady Douglas, whose loyalty was first and foremost to the coming man, Moray. Lindsay was also a member by marriage of this clan, and a more reliable jailer than Mar. The choice of Lochleven is usually connected with Moray, but it is much more likely that it was the relationship to the Douglases of the man on the spot, rather than that of the absent Moray, that led to the ad hoc decision. Moray, after all, was still abroad.

Afraid of her possible rescue by the Hamiltons, they pushed her horse to the limit. She would at least have expected to be lodged at Lochleven in the comfort that had attended her earlier, happier visits there. But on her arrival, exhausted and in despair, she was left in no doubt about her changed status. Her secretary of later years, Claude Nau, related what happened:

At the edge of the lake she was met by the Laird and his brothers, who conducted her into a room on the ground floor, furnished only with the Laird's furniture. The Queen's bed was not there, nor was there any article proper for one of her rank. In this prison, and in the midst of such desolation, Her Majesty remained for fifteen days and more without eating or drinking or conversing with the inmates of the house, so that many thought she would have died.

OPPOSITE *Mary was forced to sign her abdication under threat of death, and when weakened by a miscarriage of twins by Bothwell.*

BELOW *Patrick, Lord Ruthven, one of the two lords who accompanied Mary on the midnight ride to Lochleven following her surrender at Carberry Hill.*

Sir Robert Melville, whom she trusted, was sent on behalf of the lords to persuade her to abdicate and to divorce Bothwell, without success. But her state of mental and physical collapse was aggravated in the third week of July when she suffered a miscarriage, apparently with severe haemorrhaging. Two days later, under threat of death from Lindsay and Ruthven, and following further persuasion by Melville, she signed away the throne of Scotland to her son by means of an instrument of abdication and letters of regency in favour of Moray. It is abundantly clear that she intended to repudiate them at the earliest possible opportunity. Five days after she signed the abdication, her son was crowned at Stirling, and her host tactlessly celebrated the event by lighting bonfires and loosing off cannonades from the castle walls.

She was now moved to the main tower, to greater comfort but also greater surveillance, for two of Lady Douglas's granddaughters shared her sleeping quarters. A letter written by her to Sir Robert Melville at this time indicates her lack of creature comforts and her jailer's failure to make provision for her:

> . . . ye shall not fail to send with this bearer to me a half-ell of blue satin, and also cause Servais [the keeper of her wardrobe] to send me more twined silk if any remains, and sewing gold and sewing silver; also a doublet and skirt of white satin, another incarnat, another of black satin, and the skirts with them. Send no skirt with the red doublet. Also a loose gown of taffeta; also send the gown and other clothes that I asked Lady Lethington to send me. And also do not fail to send my maidens' clothes, for they are naked, and marvel that you have not sent them since your departure from me, together with the cambric and linen cloth of wich I gave you a memorial, and if the shoes are not ready, send them with someone else, later.

It was to be the best part of a year before this request was complied with.

From shortly after Darnley's murder Moray had been in France, cannily biding his time

ABOVE LEFT *The scholar George Buchanan enjoyed Mary's learning and lauded her during her reign. But after her fall he indicted her behaviour in his heavily biased* Detection.

ABOVE *Sir Nicholas Throckmorton, Elizabeth's envoy who had known Mary in Paris, was sent to Scotland to investigate the situation after her abdication.*

away from direct involvement in the events in Scotland until his hour came. He responded to the summons home to assume the regency with alacrity, and a fortnight later made his way to Lochleven to visit Mary. Cold and pitiless, he proceeded to give Mary a long (and not entirely undeserved) lecture on the error of her ways. On the face of it Moray's behaviour at this point seems callous, bearing in mind the generosity with which the queen had treated him in the past, but it should be remembered that most of the evidence for his ruthlessness comes from Nau. At any rate, two interviews with him proved to the queen that she could hope for nothing from him, and that all the apparent affection that had existed between them until her marriage to Darnley had gone for good. What were Moray's motives at this time? Was it the case that he had achieved a long-sought ambition, and that he would allow no personal considerations to stand in its way? Was he, the sternly religious ascetic, so appalled by her hasty marriage to his long-standing opponent Bothwell, and so convinced of her guilt in regard to Darnley's murder that he found her presence repulsive? Or did he feel that the chain of Scotland's troubles, to which link after link had been added after the fatal mistake of her marriage to Darnley, could only be snapped by him, and that he alone could restore the stability of the nation and preserve the interests of the house of Stewart?

At any rate, his attitude towards Mary at Lochleven brought with it the sharp realization that she could look for no hope of release through him. But within the house, and within the Douglas family, she began to acquire two allies: Sir William's younger brother George, and his protégé and namesake, the young Willie Douglas. They risked everything for her. George Douglas's attachment was of a romantic nature, and he seems to have had hopes of some reciprocation. What form was this to take: the queen's body, or her hand on release from imprisonment and marriage? Their closeness was perceived by Sir William, however, who banished his brother to the shore – where he continued his efforts on the prisoner's behalf. After an abortive attempt at escape, in which the queen, disguised as a washerwoman, was detected by a boatman on account of her elegant white hands, Willie Douglas, too, was temporarily despatched. But Sir William missed the foundling (who may have been his illegitimate son) and arranged for his recall.

Mary had given George Douglas a pearl earring, to be returned when the time was ripe for escape. He sent it back to her through the unwitting hands of his mother. The escape was effected through the inventiveness, the meticulous planning and the daring of the boy Willie Douglas, who seems to have been at most fourteen years of age. He arranged a feast to celebrate his return to the island, reducing the Douglases and their servants to a state of relaxation if nothing more. At dinner he served the laird personally, and carried off the most audacious element of the plan. Covering the castle keys with a napkin as they lay beside Sir William at table, he removed them and unlocked for the prisoner the gateway to the boats.

And so on the evening of 2 May 1568 Mary breached the watery defences of Lochleven and landed on the far shore, to be met by the three architects of her escape: George Douglas himself, Lord Seton, and John Beaton, a distant relative of Mary Beaton. Not far in the background was John Sempill, the husband of Mary Livingstone. From the minute she set foot on the shore her escape was made public, and she was cheered triumphantly on her way by the villagers of Kinross. Free and totally confident, her flowing hair symbolic of her condition, she led her men towards the final confrontation with Moray.

Today's visitor to the queen's place of imprisonment will find that the castle is in a state of ruination. That might be expected. But even the very island on which it stands is altered beyond recognition from those days, when its two acres only just surrounded the castle and the adjoining garden, and when the boats tied up in the shadow of the walls. In the last century drainage lowered the level of the loch, so that its area has more than doubled since the days when its perimeter was traced by the footsteps of its most famous captive.

# 14

# THE SOUTH-WEST:
# POINT OF DEPARTURE

*Dundrennan Abbey, one of the many religious foundations of the serene south-west, where Mary held her last council in Scotland.*

By 13 May Mary had built up an impressive body of support for her cause. She advanced west; and on that day encountered her half-brother's army, inferior in numbers, at Langside near Glasgow.

There is a recurrent theme in the pattern of decisive Scottish battles. It is that of the triumph of a smaller, well commanded force over a larger one whose generalship is deficient. The victories of Stirling Bridge and Bannockburn, the defeats of Flodden and Solway Moss, all conform to this pattern. Langside – Scot against Scot, Stewart against Stewart – was no exception. The generalship of Mary's chief supporters was utterly incompetent (Argyll's was so ineffectual that he was later suspected of being a fifth columnist of Moray's), and the rout of her army was complete. Dumbarton, whose strong fortress was in the loyal hands of Lord Fleming's men, would have afforded safety and a rallying point, but it was cut off by enemy troops. She headed instead for the south-west, for Galloway and Dumfriesshire, the countryside of loyal lords like Lord Herries – and the gateway to England.

She had been twice before to the south-west, perhaps the most tranquil part of her troubled kingdom. It is the most ancient cradle of Christianity in Scotland, older even than St Columba's Iona. In the fourth century, St Ninian had landed at Whithorn in Galloway and established his *Candida Casa*. His shrine became more than a mere object of pilgrimage: from it evolved a school of scholars and missionary saints. Abbeys arose along the Solway coast: Glenluce, Lincluden, Dundrennan. The most romantic of all these must be the thirteenth-century Sweetheart Abbey, founded by Devorgilla, Lady of Galloway, as a fitting resting place for the heart of her husband, John Balliol. The twentieth-century slab that now marks her grave was presented by the master and fellows of the Oxford College that bears their name, in gratitude for its seven-hundred-year history.

Mary's first visit to Galloway, in August 1563, seems to have been in the nature of a pilgrimage. In this she was following the example that had been set by her grandparents, James IV and Margaret Tudor, who had made a religious progress there. She also took advantage of the occasion to visit various important south-western lairds: Kennedy of Ardstinchar, Gordon of Lochinver, Douglas of Drumlanrig, and Maxwell of Terregles. It was an exercise in wooing friends that paid her dividends later on. The religious-cum-social nature of this progress is in sharp contrast to her visits to other far-flung parts of Scotland. Her expedition to the Highlands had been at the head of a military force; her visit to the Borders in 1566 was designed to show her in an authoritarian light. In Galloway, though the Reformation had taken hold to some extent, the religious houses had been out of the line of fire of English invasions, and were less accessible to the repercussions of momentous events at Edinburgh and St Andrews.

She appears to have visited Glenluce and Lincluden, and also St Ninian's shrine at Whithorn, which may have had an especially deep significance for her, for at Roscoff, where

firkcowbright

she had first touched the soil of France, there was another shrine to St Ninian. After a two-day visit to Kenmure House, home of Gordon of Lochinver, she made her way along the coast to Kirkcudbright, where another of Galloway's great religious houses stood: the Priory of Saint Maria de Trahil. There is no trace of the priory left on St Mary's Isle in that peaceful town, but we have a contemporary description of both town and priory, along with detailed assessments of the whole Western March and seaboard facing England, from an extensive military report made for Elizabeth I:

KIRKCUDBRIGHT four miles within the mouth of the Dee; the best post of all; ships at the ebb tide may arrive and lie within the Isle of Ross . . . and at full sea they may pass up and lie at all times under the freres of the town . . . to keep the entry of the river, the little Isle of Ross in the water's mouth may be well fortified, it is subject to a hill called Meikle Ross, but that may be helped by casting the quare of your fort and rampart next to the same higher than the rest. This Meikle Ross is but a hard ground, subject to other hills adjacent thereto. So no fort so good and able to be well fortified but only a fort of earth within St Mary's Isle, which will subject the town and river. A thousand men by sea will keep and fortify the same against all enemies. It will annoy the lairds of Lochinver, Garlies, Bounbie, Cardines and other inhabitants of Galloway on this side of the Cree, and having a garrison of 200–300 men there, it will have at your commandment, if need require, for relief of your garrison, the queen's revenues within Galloway and also the abbeys of Tauglande, Dundrennan, New Abbey, and the priory of St Mary's Isle with all the coastal fishings. They will assemble to resist you in two days, with these gentlemen before specified, in number 5100 or 5110 men, in which time you may entrench to resist that force. If you do not enterprise within as far as this St Mary's Isle, then a far lesser number will fortify the Isle of Ross at the river's mouth. It is eighteen miles distant from Workington in England, and by land from Carlisle, going straight across rivers, forty-eight miles. It will spoil their trade of wine and merchandise on that coast. . .

ABOVE *A contemporary illustration – by an English agent – of Kirkcudbright, visited by Mary during her progress in 1563.*

OPPOSITE *A portrait by Nicholas Hilliard of Mary's cousin, Queen Elizabeth, with whom she hoped to find sanctuary and support after her defeat at Langside.*

This report has been positively dated as belonging to the years between 1563 and 1566. Does it mean that Elizabeth was seriously contemplating an invasion of Scotland? If so, at what time was this considered? Could it have been after Mary's marriage to Darnley in 1565, when the rebel lords fled southwards to Elizabeth's sanctuary?

It was at that juncture that Mary paid her next visit to the area, at the head of her troops and with her new husband at her side. The rebels had concentrated their defence at Dumfries, hoping that the strong Protestant sympathies of the town would translate themselves into opposition to the queen. Personal loyalty, however, triumphed over religious zeal on the part of the key landowner of the region, John Maxwell of Terregles, and those within his sphere of influence followed his lead. Mary and Darnley entered Dumfries to find that all opposition had disappeared ignominiously across the Border. Maxwell was created Lord Herries, and from then on became one of the queen's most trusted adherents. The loyalty of the people of Dumfries was similarly unchanged by her lack of wisdom in 1567: when Moray's herald appeared at the Mercat Cross to proclaim the regency, he was hustled away by the crowd before he could issue a word of the proclamation, and only just escaped with his life.

In May of the following year, after Mary's escape from Lochleven, almost all the landowners of the south-west declared for her, and her army at Langside was made up largely of their men. The most vivid account of her flight south is told in Lord Herries' memoirs – though it should be remembered that the author was not the same Lord Herries as the committed eyewitness to the events:

So soon as the Queen saw the day was lost, she was carried from the field by Lords Herries, Fleming, and Livingstone. Pretty George Douglas and William the foundling escaped with the Queen. She rode all night, and did not halt until she came to Sanqhuar. From thence she went to Terregles, the Lord Herries' house, where she rested some days, and then, against her friends' advice, she resolved to go to England and commit herself to the protection of Queen Elizabeth; in hopes, by her assistance, to be repossessed in her kingdom.

There are many legends associated with the flight, some perhaps related to her earlier visit, and even the above statement that she stayed *some days* at Terregles cannot be accurate. She is credited with having ridden through the night, with having stayed at another house of Herries, called Corra, with having rested in a peasant cottage and been refreshed with a simple meal of oatmeal and milk. Near Tongland Bridge is the Queen's Well, reputed to have been another stop. There is no dispute, however, over the claim that it was at Dundrennan that she passed her last night in Scotland, and that she took her leave of it forever from there.

She probably stayed not in the abbey itself, if yet another legend is to be accepted, but in a private house, where she requested that the owner's small son should share her bed. Was he, in her tired mind, a substitute for her own child, nearly two years old and still at Stirling Castle, and now the unwitting focus for the ambitions of her political rivals?

Dundrennan Abbey today lies almost as ruined as those Border abbeys to the east that felt the brunt of Hertford's onslaught in the days when she too had been a pawn. But unlike them, it has a history of peaceful obscurity: even its origins are not really known. Its one brief role in affairs of state was as Mary Stuart's departure point from her kingdom: a strangely remote choice, especially given that the major port of Kirkcudbright was so near. But, as so often, closer examination reveals a link: the Commendator at the time was Lord Herries' son.

The spot from which she actually embarked, at the foot of the Abbey Burn, is called after her: Port Mary (the corresponding arrival point on the English coast being Maryport). It is difficult to reach nowadays as it is now hedged about by Ministry of Defence barriers. Even

MARIA
D          G
SCOTIÆ
PIISSIMA REGINA
FRANCIÆ DOWERIA
ANNO
ÆTATIS REGNI
36
ANGLICÆ CAPTIVA
10
S     H
1578

*Mary during her years of
English imprisonment.*

*The Solway Firth, across which Mary and a few supporters sailed to Cumbria and captivity in May 1568.*

those advisers who begged her not to take the fateful step could not have known the full horror of what was in store for her across the Solway. But as so often, she ignored wiser counsels and acted on impulse and emotion. These are qualities that may be endearing in human terms, but are disastrous politically – and, sadly for Mary, her inherited office and her own aspirations demanded the attributes of a politician.

Twenty years earlier she had set sail from Dumbarton with a fleet of galleys in grandeur and state. Her departure, forced by the ambitions and aggression of her great-uncle, Henry VIII, had been carefully planned and orchestrated by her capable and self-reliant mother. Now, in a fishing boat and with only a few companions, she was on the run from her countrymen, from her half-brother, and from the government assembled in the name of her son. Across the Firth, she fondly imagined safety and help from her cousin to be awaiting her; the harsh reality was to be nineteen years of imprisonment, and the executioner's axe.

Her reign made little physical impact on the places that had known her presence: their architecture was uninfluenced by her, nor can any permanent decoration be traced to her initiative. The bath house at Holyrood is the only surviving building for which she was responsible. On the contrary, all across the south of Scotland buildings were razed in her defence, both in her childhood years and, to a lesser extent, after she had left forever. She left some embroideries and a few poems, but no indigenous school of scholars and artists grew up around her as they had done at the courts of her father and grandfather.

But she was the embodiment of the last flourish of a Scotland whose interests were independent of those of England, as the barrenness of Henry VIII's children drew the destinies of the two nations together. Because of this, and because of all the unsolved enigmas of her actions and her character, she has left a rich but intangible legacy. Her life is a constant source of material for historical detectives, poets, novelists, dramatists and painters. And all the places associated with her in her own land are illuminated by that brief Indian summer of her personal reign as by no other part of their history.

# ACKNOWLEDGMENTS

*The authors and publishers would like to thank the following for their help in supplying illustrations and for permission to reproduce them:*

By gracious permission of Her Majesty the Queen: pp 37, 43, 136
Trustees of Blairs College: p 81 (above)
British Museum: p 73 (below)
Department of the Environment, Edinburgh: frontispiece
Mary Evans Picture Library: p 103
John Freeman (Fotomas Index): pp 15 (above), 79 (above and below), 105, 120
Galleria d'Arte Moderna, Florence (Fabri/Bridgeman Art Library): p 93
Giraudon: p 46
Guildhall Art Gallery, City of London (Bridgeman Art Library): p 73 (above)
P. Maxwell Stuart, Traquair House: pp 52 (below right), 123

Musée Condé, Chantilly (Giraudon/Bridgeman Art Library): p 47
National Galleries of Scotland: pp 16 (left and right), 25 (below), 42 (left), 50 (photo Tom Scott), 58, 60, (right), 88, 89, 96 (left), 110, 128 (left and right), 145
National Library of Scotland: pp 64–5 (above), 84 (above) 96 (right)
National Portrait Gallery: pp 60 (left), 140, 146 (left and right)
National Trust: pp 22, 84 (below, photo John Bethell), 154 (Hawkley Studios)
Private Scottish Collections: pp 30, 151
Public Record Office: pp 69, 137 (below)
Roxburgh District Council (photo Gregor Stevenson): pp 124, 144
Towneley Hall Art Gallery and Museum, Burnley (Bridgeman Art Library): p 143 (below)
Weidenfeld and Nicolson archives: p 143 (above)
All other photographs are by Eric Thorburn

# BIBLIOGRAPHY

Robert Bruce Armstrong, *The History of Liddesdale ( . . . ) and the Debatable Land*, Edinburgh 1883
M.H. Armstrong-Davison, *The Casket Letters*, London 1965
Hugo Arnot, *The History of Edinburgh*, London 1788
Sir James Balfour, *The Scots Peerage*, Edinburgh 1905
Louis A. Barbé, *Kirkcaldy of Grange*, Edinburgh and London 1897
Robert Burns Begg, *History of Lochleven Castle*, Edinburgh, 1890
Caroline Bingham, *James VI of Scotland*, London 1979
Madeleine Bingham, *Mary Queen of Scots*, London 1969
Eleanor M. Brougham, *News out of Scotland*, London 1926
P. Hume Brown, *Scotland in the Time of Queen Mary*, London 1904
Robert Chambers, *Domestic Annals of Scotland*, Edinburgh 1874
James Colston, *The Town and Port of Leith*, Edinburgh 1892
Ian B. Cowan, *The Scottish Reformation: Church and Society in Sixteenth-century Scotland*, London 1982
Ian B. Cowan & Duncan Shaw, *The Renaissance and Reformation in Scotland*, Edinburgh 1983
T. Craig Brown, *History of Selkirkshire*, Edinburgh 1886
Gordon Donaldson, *Scottish Historical Documents*, Edinburgh and London 1974
   *All the Queen's Men: Power and Politics in Mary Stewart's Scotland*, London 1983
S.R. Fraprie, *The Castles and Keeps of Scotland*, London 1908
Antonia Fraser, *Mary Queen of Scots*, London 1969
Rev. T. Crouther Gordon, *A Short History of Alloa*, London 1986
R. Gore-Browne, *Lord Bothwell*, London 1937
Elizabeth Wilson Grierson, *Edinburgh Castle, Holyrood and St Giles' Cathedral*, London 1908
Thomas Hannan, *Famous Scottish Houses: The Lowlands*, London 1928
Stuart Harris, *Mary Queen of Scots and Sir Simon Preston's House*, Edinburgh 1983
John Hill Burton, *The History of Scotland*, Edinburgh and London 1867
James Campbell Irons, *Leith and its Antiquities*, Edinburgh 1898

Helen Douglas-Irvine, *Royal Palaces of Scotland*, London 1911
David John Lee, *The Secrets of Niddrie Castle*, Thornhill 1984
Ian G. Lindsay, *Old Edinburgh*, Edinburgh 1944
Eric Linklater, *Mary Queen of Scots*, London 1937
W. Macfarlane, *Genealogical Collections*, Edinburgh 1900
D. Macgibbon & T. Ross, *Castellated and Domesticated Architecture of Scotland*, Edinburgh 1887
Agnes Mure Mackenzie, *The Scotland of Queen Mary and the Religious Wars*, London 1936
I. McPhail, *Dumbarton Castle*, Edinburgh 1979
Reginald Henry Mahon, *The Tragedy of Kirk o' Field*, Cambridge 1930
James Scott Marshall, *Life and Times of Leith*, Edinburgh 1986
Rosalind K. Marshall, *Mary of Guise*, London 1977
A.H. Millar, *Fife: Pictorial and Historical*, Cupar-Fife 1895; *Traditions and Stories of Scottish Castles*, Edinburgh and London 1947
George Scott Moncrieff, *Edinburgh*, Edinburgh 1965
Mark Powell, *Linlithgow*, Linlithgow 1974
Sir Robert Sangster Rait, *Mary Queen of Scots, 1512–1587*, London 1899
James Smith Richardson, *The Abbey of Dundrennan*, revised by C.J. Tabrahan, Edinburgh 1981
George Ridpath, *The Border History of England and Scotland*, London 1810
John Russell, *The Story of Leith*, London 1922
Tom Speedy, *Craigmillar and its Environs*, Selkirk 1892
Rev. David Steel, *St Michael's, Linlithgow*, Edinburgh 1961
A. Francis Steuart, *Seigneur Davie: A Short Life of David Riccio*, London and Edinburgh 1922
John Stuart, *A Lost Chapter in the History of Mary Queen of Scots Recovered*, Edinburgh 1874
T.D. Thomson, *Coldingham Priory*, Berwick on Tweed 1972
Nigel Tranter, *The Fortalices and Early Mansions of Southern Scotland, 1400–1650*, Edinburgh and London 1935
P.F. Tytler, *History of Scotland*, Edinburgh 1841

# INDEX

Page numbers in *italics* refer to pictures.

Abbey Burn, 153
'Abbey Lairds', 71
Aberdeen, 14, 87; University, *90*, 91
Aberdeenshire, 111
Adam brothers, 99
Agricola, Emperor, 139
Albany, John Stewart, Duke of, 17
Albany, Robert Stewart, Duke of, 77
Alexander 11, King of Scotland, 41
Alexander 111, King of Scotland, 33, 139
Allan, River, 33
Alloa, 111, 112, 113; Tower, 112–13
Ancrum Moor, 118
Angus, 88
Angus, Archibald Douglas, fifth Earl of (d. 1513), 17
Angus, Archibald Douglas, sixth Earl of, 17
Anne, Queen of Brittany, 16
Anne, Queen of England and Scotland, 79
Argyll, fifth Earl of, 107, 115, 142, 149
Argyll, Jean, Countess of, 36, 103, 107, 142
Armstrong (clan), 117, 125
Armstrong, Anthony, 117
Armstrong of Gilnockie, John, 17, 117
Arran, Countess of (sister of James 111), 51
Arran, Earl of (attainted), 51
Arran, third Earl of, 43, 49
Arran, James Hamilton, second Earl of, later Duke of Châtelherault, 25, *42*, 45, 46, 49, 59, 83, 85, 103, 109, 129, 131
Atholl, Lord (*c*.1530), 18
Atholl, Lord (1567), 137
Auldcambus, 108
Ayala, Pedro de, 15

Baillielees, 117
Balfour, Sir James, 61
Ballangleich, 39; 'Laird of', 39
Balliol College, Oxford, 149
Balliol, Edward, 141
Balliol, John, 149
Balmerino Abbey, 18, *19*, 77, 103
Bannockburn, 34, 39, 149
Barton, Sir Andrew, 50
Beaton (family), 103
Beaton, Cardinal David, Archbishop of St Andrews, 18, 43, 57, 65, 79, 80, 81, *81*, 82, 88, 92, 103
Beaton, John, 147
Beaton of Creich, Mary, 46, 71, 79, 85, 95, 103, 105, 147
Beaton of Creich, Elizabeth, 21, 103, 114
Beaton of Creich, Janet, 103, 114
Beaton of Creich, Robert, 103
Beaufort, Joan, Queen of Scotland, 24, 42, 55, 131, 135
Beaugué, de (French commander), 119
Beauly, 93

Bellenden, 117
Berker, Thomas, 135
Berwick, 49, 108
Berwickshire, 107
Biggar, 99; church, 99, *102*
Black Turnpike, 115
Blind Harry, 141
Boghall Castle, 99, *101*, 105
Bonnie Prince Charlie, *see* Stuart
Border, the, 14, 17, 28, 45, 115, 117–25, 127, 128, 129, 135, 149, 153; Lieutenants of, 123, 125, 129
Borthwick Castle, 70, 124, 129, *130*, 132, 137
Borthwickshiels, 117
Bothwell, 128; Castle, 128
Bothwell, Agnes, second Countess of (Lady Agnes Stewart), 99, 131
Bothwell, Earl of (attainted), 128
Bothwell, Francis, fifth Earl of, 131
Bothwell, James Hepburn, fourth Earl of, 13, 31, 36, 46, 59, 61, 67, 68, 69, 70, 71, 82, 83, 92, 93, 97, 101, 103, 105, 109, 111, 113, 114, 115, 120, 123, 124, 125, 127, *128*, 129, 131, 132, 135, 136, 137, 146
Bothwell, Jean, fourth Countess of (Lady Jean Gordon), 69, *128*, 131
Bothwell, Patrick Hepburn, first Earl of (first Lord Hailes), 128, 131, 135
Bothwell, Patrick Hepburn, third Earl of, 18, 43, 80, 128–9, 132
Bounbie, Laird of, 150
Brantôme, Pierre, 71
Bruce, Edward, 34
Bruce, Margery, 111
Bruce, Robert the, *see* Robert 1
Buchan, Earls of, 33
Buchanan, George, 83, 103, 124, 125, *146*
Buccleuch, Earl of, 18, 117
Bunnock, William, 22
Burghley, Lord, *see* Cecil
Burleigh Castle, 145
Burns, Robert, 13, 29
Burntisland, 83

Callendar House, 105
Campbell, Castle, 142
Capua, Prior of, 82
Carberry Hill, 61, 70, 105, 115, 124, 132, 137, *137*, 145
Cardines, Laird of, 150
Carlisle, 150
Carmichael, Elizabeth, 107
Carmichael, Euphemia, 21
Carmichael, Mary, 95
Cecil, William, later Lord Burghley, 59, 72, 87
Charles 1, King of England and Scotland, 27, 39
Charles 11, King of England and Scotland, 72
Châtelard, Pierre de, 83

Châtelherault, Duke of, *see* Arran
Clackmannan Forest, 111, 112
Clarke, Geoffrey, 29
Clyde, River, 33, 41, 45, 99
Cockburn of Henderland, Perys, 17
Cockburn of Ormiston, John, 82, 88, 129,
Coldingham, 109; Priory, 107, 108, *108*, 109, 111; Commendator of, 107, 131
Comyn family, 139
Congal, King (Pictish), 139
Congregation, the, 53, 64, 65, 97
Corra, 153
Corrichie, *86*, 92, 93, *93*
Covenanters, 39, 46
Craig, Alison, 109
Craigmillar Castle, 68, *106*, 113, *113*, 114, 115, 141
Crail, 77
Cramalt Tower, 121
Cranston, Laird of, 117
Crawford, Earls of, 88
Crawford of Jordanhill, Captain Thomas, 46, 67
Cree, River, 150
Creich Castle, *94*, 103, *104*, 105; Laird of, 103
Crichton Castle, *126*, 127, 128, 129, 131, 132
Crichton, Lord Chancellor, 56
Crichton, Sir William, 128
Crichton-Stuart family, 79
Croc, du, French ambassador, 115
Cromwell, Oliver, 61, 111
Culloden, 39
Cumberland, Duke of, 39
Cupar, 103
Cromwell, Oliver, 29

Dalgliesh, 111
Darnley, Charles, *37*
Darnley, Henry Stuart, Lord, 31, 36, *37*, 38, 39, 45, 46, 59, 61, 66, 67, 68, 69, *69*, 70, 74, 75, *84*, 85, *96*, 97, 103, 112, 114, 121, 123, 125, 131, 135, 136, 142, 145, 146, 147, 153
Dauphin of France, *see* Francis 1, Louis XI
David 1, King of Scotland, 21, 27, 70, 71, 118
David 11, King of Scotland, 56, 139, 141
Dee, River, 150
Deloraine, 117
Denmark, 51, 131, 137
Denmark, King of, 14
Devorgilla, Lady of Galloway, 149
Dingwall, 93
Dollar, 142
Douglas (family), 16, 17, 56, 77, 109, 112, 124, 125, 128, 139, 141, 145
Douglas, Archibald, *see* Angus
Douglas, David, 56
Douglas, fifth Earl of (lieutenant governor), 56
Douglas, eighth Earl of ('Black Earl'), 34

Douglas, Gavin, 14
Douglas, George, 75
Douglas, Lady Margaret, *see* Lennox
Douglas, Sir James ('Black'), 22
Douglas, Sir William, Knight of Liddesdale, 55
Douglas, William, sixth Earl of, 56
Douglas of Dalkeith, Sir Henry, 141
Douglas of Dalkeith, Sir John, 141
Douglas of Drumlanrig, 149
Douglas of Lochleven, George, 147, 153
Douglas of Lochleven, Lady (Margaret Erskine), 21, 29, 43, 145
Douglas of Lochleven, Sir Robert, 29, 139, 142
Douglas of Lochleven, Sir William, 142, 145, 147
Douglas of Lochleven, William (Willie), 147, 153
Dudley, Robert, *see* Leicester
Dumbarton, 155; Castle, 33–9, *40*, 41–6, 54, 111, 139, 149; Sheriffs of, 41, 42, 43
Dumfries, 95, 153
Dumfriesshire, 149
Dunbar, 50, 135; Castle, 70, 75, 97, 114, 121, 127, 128, 132, *134*, 135, 136, 137,
Dunbar, Lady ('Black Agnes'), 135
Dunbar, William, 14
Dundee, 77, *78*
Dundrennan Abbey, *148*, 149, 150, *152*, 153; Commendator of, 153
Dunfermline, 21; Abbey, 54, 109, 141
Durham, 107, 108
Dryburgh, 118

East Linton, 132
Edgar, King of Scotland, 107
Edinburgh, 49, 53, 55, 56, 61, 63–75, *66*, 83, 85, 87, 92, 97, 101, 105, 113, 115, 120, 125, 127, 135, 136, 137, 145, 149; Castle, 33, *48*, 49–61, *55*, 63, 70, 99, 101, 111, 112, 113, 131, 135, 139; map, *64–5*; Provosts of, 97, 114; Sheriff Principal of, 128; University, 29, *67*, 68
Edinburghshire, 55
Edward I, King of England, 21, 33, 41, 88, 135
Edward II, King of England, 34, 55
Edward III, King of England, 34, 55, 141
Edward VI, King of England, 36
Edzell Castle, 88, 89
Elboeuf, Marquis d' (Guise), 109, 131
Eldinhope, 117
Elgin Cathedral, 92
Elliot (clan), 123, 125
Elliot of the Park, Jock, 123
Elizabeth I, Queen of England, 31, 36, 38, 49, 60, 61, 72, 85, 97, 103, 129, 150, *151*, 153
Elizabeth, Queen, the Queen Mother, 88
England, 13, 14, 16, 31, 33–4, 42, 49, 65, 75, 105, 111, 117, 129, 132, 137, 149, 150, 153, 155
Erskine (family), 111, 112,
Erskine, Lord (guardian of James v), 112
Erskine, fifth Lord, 36, 111, 112

Erskine, sixth Lord, *see* Mar
Erskine, Margaret, *see* Douglas of Lochleven
Erskine, Robert de, 111
Esse, Monsieur d', 45
Essenside, 118
Esk, Rivers, 114
Ettrick, 117; Forest, 117, *118* (map), 121, *122*
Eure, General Sir Ralph, 117, 118

Falkirk, 39, 105
Falkland Palace, *12*, 17, 25, *76*, 77, 79, 85, 103
Ferguson, Dr John, 29
Fife, 25, 50, 77, 82, 83, 85, 103, 108, 112, 114, 141
Flanders, 14, 24, 57,
Fleming, Janet, Lady, 45, 99
Fleming, John, fourth Lord, 101
Fleming, Malcolm, third Lord, 99, 101
Fleming, fifth Lord, 46, 149, 153
Fleming, Mary (later Lady Maitland of Lethington), 46, 71, 95, 96, 99, 101, 103, 107, 131, 146
Flodden, 16, 17, 24, 25, 34, 96, 99, 101, 109, 112, 129, 149
Forester, William, 117
Forfar, 88
Forster, Robert, 117
Forth, River, 33, 50, 85, 99, 111, 112, 113, 114
Foster (clan), 118
Foster, John, 117
Foster, Robin, 118
France, 13, 14, 17, 18, 21, 34, 41, 42, 43, 45, 46, 49, 54, 58, 65, 77, 79, 82, 83, 96, 97, 99, 103, 105, 107, 111, 114, 129, 131, 137, 150
Francis I, King of France, 18
Francis II, King of France (also as Dauphin), 31, 45, 46, 49, 53, 57, 71, 96, 99, 101, 114

Galloway, 57, 149, 150
Garlies, Laird of, 150
Gaunt, John of, 24
Geneva, 65, 82,
George IV, King of the United Kingdom, 75
Glamis Castle, 88
Glasgow, 14, 68, 99, 115, 128, 149; Archbishop of, 75
Glenluce Abbey, 149
Gordon (family), 87, 92
Gordon, Alexander, 90–91
Gordon, George, *see* Huntly
Gordon, Lady Jean, *see* Bothwell
Gordon, Sir John, 87, 91
Gordon of Lochinver, 149, 150, 151
Graham clan, 117, 118
Granton, 53
Grey of Winton, Lord, 132
Guise (family), 19, 41, 49, 111
Guise, Duke Francis of, 85
Guise, Renée de, 99
*see also* Elboeuf, Mary of Guise

Haddington, 45, 80, 129
Hailes Castle, 127, 128, 132, *133*
Hailes, second Lord, 131
Hailes, Patrick, first Lord, *see* Bothwell

Hamilton (family), 145
Hamilton, James, *see* Arran
Hamilton, Mary, 95
Hamilton, Sir Patrick, 57
Hamilton of Bothwellhaugh, James, 29, 31
Hans (a Dutch builder), 135
Hawick, 13, 120
Helmburn, 117
Henri II, King of France, 45
Henry II, King of England, 33
Henry III, King of England, 139
Henry IV, King of England, 22
Henry VI, King of England, 22
Henry VII, King of England, 14
Henry VIII, King of England, 16, 19, 24, 25, 34, 36, 43, 45, 53, 112, 117, 129, 155
Henry, Prince, 39
Hepburn (family), 125, 127, 128, 131, 135
Hepburn, Bishop of Elgin, 92
Hepburn, James, *see* Bothwell
Hepburn, Lady Janet, 111, 131
Hermitage Castle, 13, *116*, 120–21, 123, 124–5, 128
Herries, Lord (author of memoirs), 60, 153
Herries, Lord (John Maxwell of Terregles, Master of Maxwell), 149, 153
Hertford, Earl of, *see* Somerset
Highlands, 17, 18, 33, 87, 88, 93, 149; and islands, 13, 14
Holyrood Abbey, 70–71; Commendator of, 109; Palace, 25, 57, 59, 61, 62, 63, 65, 68, 69, 70, *70–71*, 71, 72, 74, *74*, 75, 81, 83, 93, 97, 103, 105, 114, 115, 121, 132, 137, 145, 155
Home family, 109
Hope family, 99
Hopetoun House, 99
Howpaslet, 117
Hume, lairds of, 18, 128
Huntly, 117
Huntly, Countess of, 91, 93
Huntly, fourth Earl of (George Gordon, d. 1562), 64, 87, 88, *88*, 91, 92
Huntly, fifth Earl of, 67, 93, 97, 115, 124, 135
Huntly, Earls of, 92
Hurly Haaky Hill, 34

Inchmahome Priory, 13, *35*, 36; Commendator of, 29
Innerleithen, 121
Inverness, 93, 111; Castle, 91
Iona, 139, 149
Ireland, 41
Italy, 24

James I, King of Scotland, 22, 42, 56, 88, 107, 128, 135
James II, King of Scotland, 34, 51, 56, 57, 114, 135
James III, King of Scotland, 34, 51, 128
James IV, King of Scotland, 14–16, *16*, 17, 21, 24, 27, 28, 34, 49, 50, 57, 71, 72, 95, 99, 103, 107, 109, 112, 128, 135, 149
James V, King of Scotland, 16–18, *16*, 19, 21, 22, 24, 25, 29, 31, 34, 39, 45, 57, 69, 77, *77*, 79, 107, 112, 115, 117, 120, 129, 142

James VI, King of Scotland, and I of England, 27, 31, 36, 38–9, 59–61, *60*, 70, 75, 88, 99, 103, 105, 113, 137, 146
Jedburgh (Jeddart, Jethart), 13, 119, 123, 124, *124*, 145; Abbey, 118
John, King of England, 108

Keats, John, 13
Kellie, 111
Kelso, 108, 125; Abbey, 118
Kenmure House, 150
Kennedy, Jane, 99
Kennedy of Ardstinchar, 149
Kerr (family), 17, 118, 119, 121, 125
Kerr of Ferniehirst (family), 125
Kinross, 139, 141, 145, 147
Kirk o'Field, 68, 75, 103, 115, 124, 136
Kirkcaldy of Grange, Sir William, 61, 80, 88, 137
Kirkcudbright, 150, *150*, 153
Kirkhope, 117
Knox, John, 29, 31, 57, 63, 64, 65, 66, 67, 71, 72, 80, 82, 83, 88, 105, 111, 114, 142, *143*

Langside, 31, 46, 61, 97, 149, 153
Lareyneville, de, or Gryssoner, Joanna, 103
Latoun, General Sir Brian, 117, 118
Leicester, Robert Dudley, Earl of, 74, 85,
Leith, 49, 50, 51, *51*, 53, 54, 55, 57, 71
Lennox, Countess of (Lady Margaret Douglas), 43, *43*, 45, 85, 142
Lennox, Earl of (Sir John Menteith), 41
Lennox, Malcolm, Earl of, 42
Lennox, Matthew, fourth Earl of, 31, 39, *42*, 43, 45, 46, 61, 69, 85, *136*
Leslie, John, Bishop of Ross, 101
Leslie, Norman, 80
Leslie of Parkhill, John, 80
Lethington, Laird of, *see* Maitland
Liddesdale, 117, 119, 121, 124, *124*, 125, 127, 129
Lilliard, Fair Maiden, 118
Lincluden Abbey, 149
Lindsay, Lord, 145, 146
Linlithgow, 22, *22*, 27, 29, 33; Palace, *20*, 21–9, *22*, 24–*5*; St Michael's Church, *20*, 21, *22*, 24, *26*, 27, 28–9, 54
Livingstone, Lord (regent for James II), 56
Livingstone, fourth Lord, 105
Livingstone, fifth Lord, 36, 105
Livingstone, sixth Lord, 153
Livingstone, Mary, 46, 71, 95, 96, 105, 147
Lochinver, Laird of, *see* Gordon of Lochinver
Lochleven: Castle, 61, 97, 137, *138*, 139–47, 153; Lairds of, 121, 141, *see also* Douglas of Lochleven
London, 39, 41, 50, 75
Lord High Admiral, 128
Lothians, the, 50, 95, 107, 127, 128, 129, 132, 137
Louis XI, King of France (as Dauphin), 42
Low Countries, 14, 49, 51, 57
Lowlands, 33, 121
Lyndsay, Sir David, 17, 25, *25*, 64, 80

Macbeth, King of Scotland, 88, 139
Madeleine, Princess of France and Queen of Scotland, 18, 77, 107
Maitland of Lethington, Lady, *see* Fleming, Mary
Maitland of Lethington, Sir William, 72, 87, 101, 103, *103*, 115, 124
Malcolm III Canmore, King of Scotland, 54
Mar (family), 112, 113
Mar, Earl of (1562–5), *see* Moray
Mar, Earls of, 87, 111
Mar, John, Earl of (1547), 36
Mar, John, Earl of (from 1565; formerly sixth Lord Erskine), 38, 39, 61, *110*, 112, 113, 145
Marches, the : West and Middle, Warden of, 128; Western, 150
Margaret (Stuart), Princess, 42
Margaret (Windsor), Princess, 88
Margaret, Queen of Scotland, 54, 71
Margaret of Denmark, Queen of Scotland, 51
Margaret Plantagenet, Queen of Scotland, 139
Margaret Tudor, Queen of Scotland, 14, 17, 24, 27, 28, 71, 85, 109, 128, 129, 149
'Maries', 'the four', 71, 95–105, 107, 145; *see also* Beaton, Fleming, Livingstone, Seaton
Mary of Guise or Lorraine, Princess of France and Queen of Scotland, 18, 29, 21, *22*, 25, 19, 31, 34, 36, 43, 45, 46, 49, 53, 57–9, *58*, 65, 77, 79, 81, 82, 95, 96, 103, 105, 107, 114, 118, 127, 129, 131
Mary of Guelders, Queen of Scotland, 43, 51, 56, 131
Mary, Princess, 43
Mary, Queen of Scots: birth and infancy at Linlithgow, 21–9, 34; childhood and youth at Stirling, 33–9, at Dumbarton, 41–6, and in France, 45–6, 49; coronation of, 34; court of, 17, 25, 103; marriages to Francis II, 45, 56, 57, 101, 131, to Darnley, 31, 36, 46, 59, 66, 67, 68, 74, 75, 85, 97, 112, 115, 121, 123, 125, 131, 135, 147, 153, and to Bothwell, 13, 31, 46, 59, 61, 69, 70, 71, 97, 101, 105, 113, 115, 124, 127, 132, 136, 137, 146; miscarriage, 146; portraits, *frontispiece*, *47*, *50*, *84*, *96*, *120*, *140*, *143*, *144*, *154*; principal houses visited by, 107–14; religious disputes, 65–7, 87, 142; return to Scotland and time at Edinburgh Castle, 49–61, 97, 131, and Holyrood, 59, 65, 68–75; royal progresses through Fife, 77–85, the north, 87–93, and the Borders, 121–5; son (James VI), birth of, 36, 38–9, 59–61, 68, 107, 112; surrender, abdication and imprisonment, 61, 66, 70, 99, 132, 137, 138, 145–6, 155; vain escape and final defeat, 147, 149, 153, 155
Mary Tudor, Queen of England, 65
Maryport, 153
Master of the King's Household, 128
Maxwell, Master of (under James V), *18*
Maxwell, Mr or Master, 129
Maxwell of Terregles, John (the Master of Maxwell), *see* Herries

Megget (-dale, -land), 121
Melrose Abbey, *15*, 118, *119*, 123, 124,
Melville, Sir James, 60
Melville, Sir Robert, 146
Menteith, Earls of, 33, 36
Menteith, Lake of, 13, *35*, 36
Menteith, Sir John, 36, 41
Merlione, Walter, 135
Merse, the, 127
Midgehope, 117
Moray, Bishop of, 92
Moray, Countess of, 142
Moray, first Earl of (also Earl of Mar, Lord James Stewart), 28, 29, *30*, 31, 36, 46, 49, 54, 68, 72, 74, 75, 82, 83, 85, 87–8, *89*, 93, 107, 111, 113, 115, 119, 120, 121, 123, 124, 125, 129, 131, 137, 141, 142, 145, 146–7, 149, 153
Moray, Randolph, Earl of, 54, 55
Moretta, de, Savoyard ambassador, 68, 72
Morton, Earl of, *60*, 61

Nau, Claude, 124, 145, 147
Nesbit, 111
New Abbey, 150
Newhaven, 49
Niddry Castle, 97, 99, *100*, 105
Northumbria, 107
Norway, 49, 137

Ogilvie of the Boyne, Alexander, 103
Orkney, 51, 137; Lord of, 128
Orme, David, 82

Paris, 101
Paris (Mary's servant), 68
Peebles, 121, 123
Peffermill House, 115
Perth, 77, 88
Peter the Great, King of Russia, 95
Picardy, 103
Pieris, Marie, 96
Pinkie Cleugh, 13, 36, *44*, 45, 53, 101, 129, 142
Pitscottie, Robert Lindsay of, 25
Pope Pius IV, 72
Port Mary, 153
Preston of Craigmillar (family), 114
Preston of Craigmillar, Sir Simon, 113, 114, 115, 136, 145
Preston of Craigmillar, William, 114

Queen's Mire, 125
Queen's Well, 153

Randolph, Sir Thomas, 22, 59, 72, 74, 85, 88, 91, 101, 103, 111, 121, 131
Reres, Margaret, Lady, 103
Restalrig, 53, 57, 71
Rheims, 99
Richard I, King of England, 33
Rizzio, David, 31, 38, 59, 68, 70, 72, *73*, 75, 81, 82, 83, 93, 97, 103, 112, 114, 121, 132, 137
Robert I Bruce, King of Scotland, 21, 22, 33, 34, 42, 54, 79, 95, 111

Robert II, King of Scotland, 111, 141
Robert III, King of Scotland, 22, 56, 77
Robert, Prince (Malcolm Canmore's brother), 54
Romans, 41
Roscoff, 149
Ross, Duke of, 17
Ross, Euphemia, 141
Ross, Isle of, 150
Rothes, Earl of, 80
Rothesay, Duke of, 77
Roxburgh, 111
Roxburgh Castle, 57
Russia, 95
Ruthven, Patrick, Lord, 75, 145, 146

Sadler, Sir Ralph, 82
Salisbury, Earl of, 135
St Andrews, 14, 79, 82–3, *83*, 85, 131, 149; Archbishops of, 16, 18, 39, 109, 141; Castle, 79, 80, *81*, 82, *82*, 83, 88; Cathedral, 27; Commendator of, 29, 82; map, *84*; University of, 65, 79
St Columba, 139, 149
St Giles, 114
St Giles' Cathedral, Edinburgh, 61, 64–5, *64–5*, 66, 67, 70, 114
St Maria de Trahil, Priory of, 150
St Mary's Isle, 150
St Michael's Church, *see* Linlithgow
St Ninian, 149
St Patrick, 41
St Ronan, 139
St Serf, 139
Scone, 88, 139
Scotland: France, relations with, 18, 19, 29, 31, 39, 45, 58, 72, 81–2, 135; map, *15*, national status of, 13–14, 17, 42, 155; Reformation in, 27, 49, 53, 54, 58, 63, 65, 79, 82, 88, 93, 99, 109, 119, 129, 149; union of, 41, 54; union with England, 31, 39, 55, 91; wars with England, 21–2, 33–4, 36, 42, 45, 50, 53, 54, 55, 57, 71, 95, 108, 112, 117–19, 129, 132, 135, 137, 141, 152
Scott (clan), 17, 117, 119, 121, 123, 137
Scott, Sir Walter, 27, 75, 132
Scott of Buccleuch, Sir Walter, 125
Selkirk, 117, 118, 123
Sempill, John, 105, 147,
Sempill, Lord, 105
Servais (wardrobe keeper), 146

Seton, 75, 95; House, 97, *98*, 105, 132
Seton (family), 95–9, *96*
Seton, Christopher, 95
Seton, George, fifth Lord, 96, 97, 99, 101
Seton, second Lord, 95–6
Seton, third Lord, 96, 99
Seton, fifth Lord, 96, 97, 99, 147
Seton, Mary, 71, 95, 96, 99, 105, 114
Seye, Secker de, 95
Shaw of Sauchie, Elizabeth, 21
Shawe, John, 145
Shawe, William, 145
Shaws, 117
Shetland, 51; Lord of, 128
Siena, 131
Sinclair, Lady Agnes, *see* Bothwell
Sinclair, Lord, 14
Sinclair, Oliver, 25
Singlie, 118
Solway Firth, 155, *155*
Solway Moss, 25, 79, 149
Somerset, Duke of (Earl of Hertford), 36, 45, 46, 53, 57, 97, 114, 153
Soulis, de (family), 124
Soulis, Lord, 125
Spain, 16
Spynie Palace, *91*, 92, 137
Stanley, Sir William, 60
Stewart (House of), 111, 131, 147
Stewart, Alexander, 109
Stewart, Bishop David, 92
Stewart, Elizabeth, 21
Stewart, Francis, 111
Stewart, Henry, *see* Darnley
Stewart, John, *see* Albany
Stewart, Lady Agnes, *see* Bothwell
Stewart, Lord James, *see* Moray
Stewart, Lord John, 107, 109, 111, 131
Stewart, Lord Robert, 107, 109
Stewart, Robert, 34; *see also* Albany
Stewart of Traquair, Sir John, 121, 123
*See also* Stuart, Christian names of Stuart monarchs
Stirling, 77; Bridge, 33, 149; Castle, 17, 21, 25, *32*, 33–9, *38–9*, 54, 57, 70, 111, 112, 137, 139, 145, 146, 153
Stirling of Glorat, George, 45
Stonehaven, 91
Story, Edward, 117
Strathbogie, 91
Strathclyde, 41

Strathmore, Patrick, first Earl of, 88
Stryvelyne, Sir John, 141
Stuart, Charles Edward (Bonnie Prince Charlie), 27, 39, 75, 93
Stuart, Henry, *see* Darnley
    *see also* Stewart, Christian names of Stewart monarchs
Surrey, Earl of, 16
Sweetheart Abbey, 149

Tauglande Abbey, 150
Tay, River, 77
Taylor (Darnley's servant), 68
Teith, River, 33
Terregles, 153
Teviot, River, 120
Teviotdale, 117, 125
Thirlestane, 117
Throckmoton, Sir Nicholas, *146*
Throndsen, Anna, 131, 137
Tongland Bridge, 153
Traprain Law, 132
Traquair House, *52*, 121, *122*, 123
Tudor, House of, 17, 31, 36
Tweed, River, 16, 99, 121
Tweeddale, 121
Tyne, River, 127, 132

Valois, House of, 41
Vendôme, Duchess of, *see* Mary of Guise
Vendôme, Duke of, 19, 21
Virgil, 14

Wallace, Sir William, 22, 33, 36, 41, 42, 141
Walter the Steward, 111
Warbeck, Perkin, 14
Wemyss Castle, 85
Wharton, Lord, 117
Whitehillbraes, 117
Whithorn, 149
William the Lion, King of Scotland, 33, 121
Winchburgh, 95
Winton, Andrew, 139, 141
Wishart, George, 65, 79, 80, *80*, 129, 132
Wood, Sir Andrew (1496), 135
Wood, Sir Andrew (c.1700), 50
Workington, 150
Wright, Peter and Janet, 99

Yoletta, Queen of Scotland, 33